OSPREY COMBAT AIRC

IRANIAN
F-4 PHANTOM II
UNITS IN COMBAT

SERIES EDITOR: TONY HOLMES

OSPREY COMBAT AIRCRAFT • 37

IRANIAN F-4 PHANTOM II UNITS IN COMBAT

Farzad Bishop and Tom Cooper

OSPREY
PUBLISHING

Front cover
Early on 26 April 1981, four F-4Es of the Islamic Republic of Iran Air Force's 34th Tactical Fighter Squadron (TFS) attacked the Iraqi air base of Ubaydah Ibn-Jarrah. After successfully bombing the target, the formation was intercepted by four Iraqi fighters – two MiG-21s and two MiG-23s. Using the F-4's APX-80 'Combat Tree' enemy identification friend/foe (IFF) interrogator equipment and TISEO (Target-identification System, Electro-optical) telescopic camera, the Phantom II crews swiftly detected the approaching fighters and successfully out-manoeuvred them. One of the Iranian pilots involved in this action was Capt Mahlouji, who later reported;

'Thanks to "Combat Tree" and the TISEO, we knew for sure that two Iraqi MiG-23s were ahead of us, so we went after them with our radars off. The flight leader ordered me to keep my eyes open for the MiG-21s that we knew were nearby. As we closed on the two MiG-23s from behind, it appeared they had not seen us, and were focused on something else. The leader had just begun to get a missile tone from his Sidewinder when his WSO (Weapons System Officer) warned him that an F-4E from the other pair had cut in between us and the Iraqi MiGs. As the other Phantom II passed by, I reported "Close" to my leader to let him know he was covered by me. He responded, "Stay as close as possible", while trying to turn hard to starboard to stay behind the MiG-23s.

'As I followed his turn, a single MiG-21 suddenly rolled out 100 metres away from my leader, who had, meanwhile, initiated a left turn, tracking the two MiG-23s ahead of him. With a clear target in front of me, I quickly fired a single Sidewinder. The Iraqi had no time to manoeuvre. The missile hit, and a red and white fireball covered its tail area. The jet crashed nose-down into the ground below.

'The leader then reacquired the MiG-23s with the help of the TISEO, and after some very hard manoeuvring, shot one of the Iraqi jets down using Sidewinders. There were now more MiGs in the area, but we decided to disengage, clearing our "six" and turning back east. A bombed Iraqi airfield and two MiGs were enough for one day – the war was still far from over' (*Cover artwork by Mark Postlethwaite*)

First published in Great Britain in 2003 by Osprey Publishing
Elms Court, Chapel Way, Botley, Oxford, OX2 9LP

© 2003 Osprey Publishing Limited

ISBN 1 84176 658 5

Edited by Tony Holmes and Bruce Hales-Dutton
Page design by Tony Truscott
Cover artwork by Mark Postlethwaite
Aircraft profiles by Jim Laurier
Scale drawings by Mark Styling
Index by Alan Thatcher
Origination by Grasmere Digital Imaging, Leeds, UK
Printed by Stamford Press PTE Ltd, Singapore

EDITOR'S NOTE
To make this best-selling series as authoritative as possible, the Editor would be interested in hearing from any individual who may have relevant photographs, documentation or first-hand experiences relating to the world's elite pilots, and their aircraft, of the various theatres of war. Any material used will be credited to its original source. Please write to Tony Holmes via e-mail at:
tony.holmes@osprey-jets.freeserve.co.uk

For a catalogue of all Osprey Publishing titles please contact us at:

Osprey Direct UK, PO Box 140, Wellingborough, Northants NN8 2FA, UK
E-mail: info@ospreydirect.co.uk

Osprey Direct USA, c/o MBI Publishing, 729 Prospect Ave, PO Box 1, Osceola, WI 54020, USA
E-mail: info@ospreydirectusa.com

CONTENTS

INTRODUCTION

Pugnacious, bent-winged and hook-nosed, the McDonnell Douglas F-4 Phantom II looked dangerous even when at rest on the ground. And its combat record was to show that looks did not deceive, for whether shooting down MiGs, providing a bulwark for the West against the Soviet bloc or fighting daily battles in Israeli service over the Middle East, the Phantom II was seldom out of the news.

During the 1960s and well into the 1970s, the F-4 represented the very latest in military technology, and it remained capable of giving a good account of itself well into the 1980s. Indeed, around a fifth of the 5100 Phantom IIs built are still in active service as this volume goes to press.

In addition to its power, a key Phantom II attribute was its versatility, the F-4 providing more than a dozen air arms with their first taste of multi-role, Mach 2 capability. Inevitably, such ability came at a price – complexity. And it was this complexity which many analysts and observers considered would prove too much for the Islamic Republic of Iran Air Force (IRIAF), cut off from US support after the 1979 revolution. Events were to prove them wrong, however, for during the war with Iraq, Iran's Phantom IIs were not only operated effectively, but were kept flying, often under highly adverse circumstances, by their groundcrews.

Despite myriad publications that have detailed the Phantom II's development and service history over the past four decades, the aircraft's part in the Iran-Iraq War remains shrouded in mystery. The Shah's air force represented the second biggest export customer for the F-4 after Israel, but there are more questions than answers about the way the aircraft were operated after the 1979 Islamic Revolution. Inevitably, these questions have provoked much rumour but little hard fact on how many units actually remained operational during the conflict, the standard of the equipment employed in combat, who flew these jets and the number of F-4s that survived.

Given the secrecy which veiled the Iranian Phantom IIs right from the start, this is hardly surprising. Even today, it is not entirely clear how many F-4s were actually delivered. Much of the equipment was classified even in US service, and the deterioration in relations between America and Iran since the Islamic revolution has made it hard for many to believe that Iranian Phantom IIs were equipped with 'full-standard' avionics and weapon systems. Some items of equipment were 'top of the line', while others had to be handled under carefully controlled conditions.

Many Iranian pilots were trained in the US, or by American instructors temporarily based in Iran, and given the frigid relations which subsequently developed between the two countries, it is perhaps hard to recognise the level of friendship and mutual respect which sprung up between the Americans and their students prior to the revolution. Similarly, the early successes of the Iranian Phantom II pilots in their first combat sorties against Iraq in 1974-75 , as well as against rebels in Oman, have been almost completely forgotten.

The end result of all this secrecy has been the circulation of wild theories pertaining to the employment, and operability, of Iranian Phantoms II. Some observers have suggested that they were delivered with a low standard of equipment, and that pilots and groundcrew were so hastily trained that they never managed to fully understand the complexity of the aircraft. Inevitably, such stories were influenced by reports of purges of Iranian officers and pilots – even executions – carried out during and after the Islamic Revolution. As a result of all these theories, Western observers believed that the availability of Iranian Phantom IIs was very low – 'there are only 20 to 30 remaining examples languishing in a sad state of disrepair' has been the standard line that has appeared in numerous defence-related publications over the past 20 years.

It was also often suggested that the best and most capable personnel had left the country, leaving the 'new' IRIAF unable to effectively maintain and operate such an advanced aircraft.

This situation, many thought, was unlikely to change with the out-break of war between Iraq and Iran. Despite the presence of Phantom IIs over Baghdad, international press reports continued to focus on the poor condition of the aircraft, the lack of spares and the shortage of trained pilots. Rumours suggested that the Iranian F-4s were to be re-equipped with Rolls-Royce Spey engines, that some spares were being supplied secretly by Israel and certain NATO countries, and that others were being provided clandestinely by the US in exchange for American hostages held in Lebanon. Apart from being largely incorrect, all these reports obscured the truth about what was really happening. Observers were quick to 'write off' the F-4s, just as they had the Iranian Grumman F-14A Tomcats.

This book is an attempt to set the record straight, and to tell the true story of the way the Iranian Phantom IIs were used during the war with Iraq. It features numerous first-hand accounts by the pilots who flew different versions of the aircraft during the long and bloody war in the Middle East. The story shows that the Iranian pilots operated under unbelievably difficult circumstances and against all odds, being short of support, advanced weapons, regular maintenance, spare parts and, crucially, political and tactical support. In fact, Iranian pilots were under severe pressure from the new religious regime in Tehran.

Originally branded 'disloyal elements' by Islamic fundamentalists, the pilots' patriotism and expertise were completely ignored. Indeed, they were regarded as 'expendable', and many were imprisoned, tortured and executed during the chaos of the early revolutionary days. Nevertheless, they remained what they were – pilots who loved flying, and who cherished their aircraft. When war broke out they were forced to defend their country on pain of jail or execution. They would have done it anyway because it was their duty.

Yet the heroism and ingenuity of the Iranian Phantom II pilots and their support personnel has remained virtually unknown until now. In the pages which follow, a small but dedicated and proud group of surviving pilots and technicians speak out to tell their story.

Farzad Bishop & Tom Cooper,
Austria, April 2003

IRAN's PHANTOM IIs

In 1980 the fledgling Islamic Republic of Iran Air Force (IRIAF) was still in a state of deep shock. The Islamic Revolution, which had ousted Mohamad Reza Shah Pahlavi from power in February 1979, had resulted in a dismembered leadership structure. Officers and pilots were lost to frequent politically motivated – and senseless – purges, with defections, forced retirements and imprisonments commonplace. There were even some executions. Yet despite this, it was still a huge air force.

In late 1978 the Imperial Iranian Air Force boasted no less than 520 modern combat aircraft, most of which were brand new, plus 100 transports and some 60 helicopters. Personnel numbered 100,000, of which 5000 were qualified pilots. Before the revolution, it had been planned to qualify up to 100 new fighter pilots per month, and to introduce the 300 F-16A/Bs which had been ordered in 1976-77. Yet by the summer of 1980 the IRIAF was in a complete state of chaos.

Even after changing its name from the Imperial Iranian Air Force (IIAF) to the Islamic Republic of Iran Air Force, and almost halving the number of active personnel, the new regime was deeply suspicious of a service which the Shah had been so proud of, and whose personnel had been loyal to the deposed leader.

Simultaneously, the new regime started to antagonise Iran's principal ally, the USA. Many in the revolutionary government could not understand the need to maintain so many complex and expensive aircraft in such a huge and costly service. 'What do we need them for?' was a question frequently heard in Iran at the time, to be followed by the statement, 'we do not want to attack anybody'.

But such questions were soon to be answered. Even if the Iranians did not plan on attacking their neighbours, they themselves were about to be attacked. Soon enough, the IRIAF would be called upon to play the decisive role of defending Iran. All the aircraft purchased at such huge cost – and especially the F-4s – would prove their worth beyond any doubt.

In 1980, Iran had three different versions of the Phantom II in service. Its inventory included 29 F-4Ds, 162 F-4Es and at least 17 (perhaps as many as 19) RF-4Es. They formed the backbone of the air force.

With the renaming of the Iranian air force came the adoption of a new symbol – a Phoenix. However, the IRIAF was only partly 'new', for its structure had not changed, and nor was it to change even after eight long years of war with Iraq, regardless of the number of aircraft lost in combat. Of course, some squadrons operated from temporary bases during the war, while others had to be partially evacuated for short periods, even if they remained operational, when their bases came under fire from Iraqi artillery shells and Luna/FROG-7 surface-to-surface rockets. In general,

F-4D 67-14874 was the fifth Phantom II built for Iran, and it is seen here prior to its delivery whilst still wearing US markings (*US DoD*)

F-4D 67-14870 was the second Phantom II supplied to Iran, and the jet is seen here shortly after its delivery to the IIAF. Note the SUU-23/A gun pod mounted on the aircraft's centreline. This weapon was standard equipment for the F-4D during the Iran-Iraq War (*US DoD*)

though, after the revolution, and for the next ten years, almost everything in connection with F-4s in Iranian service remained as it had been in 1978.

THE PHANTOM II ARRIVES

The F-4D was the first version delivered to Iran, with 32 examples arriving between 1968 and 1970. By 1980, up to 29 remained in service with two units, the 306th and the 308th TFSs, both of which were under the control of the 32nd Tactical Fighter Wing (TFW) at Nojeh air base (formerly Shahrokhi), near Hamedan. Like other major IIAF air bases, Nojeh was given a designation as a tactical fighter base (TFB), with a number applied in chronological order depending on the time it was declared operational. Nojeh was the third largest base at which flying units were permanently based, and it was designated TFB 3.

By 1979, the F-4D was considered a 'second-line' asset, despite the addition of advanced equipment which included laser-designators and laser-guided bombs, as well as advanced RHAWS (Radar Homing and Warning System). This was to change as soon as the war with Iraq started.

The F-4E was the version best equipped to meet Iranian needs. It was also the most numerous, with 177 newly-built examples being supplied by the USA between 1971 and 1978 – some 162 were officially still in service in 1980. There is also a possibility that a few USAF examples that were sent to Iran in advance of new jets arriving in the Middle East were also left behind, although official sources maintain that all the leased aircraft were returned before the revolution.

By 1978 Iranian F-4Es had been upgraded through the addition of leading edge slats and the avionics associated with the Mod 556 front and rear cockpits. Some 50 jets were also equipped with the ASX-1 TISEO electro-optical sensor, and, crucially, more than 80 had been fitted with the state of the art APX-70 'Combat Tree' IFF interrogator system.

TACTICAL DEPLOYMENT

The following tactical fighter squadrons operated the F-4E in September 1980:

– 11th and 12th TFSs of the 11th TFW at Tehran-Mehrabad (TFB 1)

– 61st and 62nd TFSs of the 61st TFW (CO Col Dadpay) at Bushehr (TFB 6), flying TISEO/Maverick-capable F-4Es

– 91st 'Sharks' and 92nd TFSs of the 91st TFW (CO Col A Zowghi) at Bandar Abbas (TFB 9), operating F-4Es delivered to Iran in 1978

– 71st and 72nd TFSs of the 71st TFW (CO Maj Daneshmandi), flying TISEO-equipped aircraft from Shiraz TFB 7 (base commanded by Gen Seyed-Javadi). Soon after the start of the war with Iraq, both of these units swapped their F-4Es for the F-4Ds of the 306th and 308th TFSs of the 32nd TFW (CO Lt Col Golchin), based at Nojeh (TFB 3)

– 31st, 32nd and 33rd TFSs of the 31st TFW, also based at Nojeh. These units initially flew the F-4E, but as the war developed, it was considered that the F-4Ds would be more useful on the southern front, where they could deploy their laser-guided bombs (LGBs) against various Iraqi targets (particularly bridges) to good effect. At the same time, a concentration of four F-4E units at centrally-positioned Nojeh would give the IRIAF the ability to react swiftly to any threat along the frontline, or mount interdiction strikes virtually anywhere in Iraq, using aerial refuelling, even if ordered at short notice

– 101st TFS was based at Chabahar, in south-eastern Iran, but its aircraft were sent as replacements to frontline units soon after the outbreak of war. The unit was reactivated with F-4Ds post-war

This force structure and base allocation was maintained for the duration of the Iran-Iraq War, although a squadron of F-4Es from the 31st TFW was later deployed to Vahdati (TFB 4), near Dezful, and aircraft from the 91st TFW were sent to reinforce other units in western Iran. Some F-4Ds were constantly moved around to other bases as required, and it seems that a number of these detachments were known by their old squadron designations. For example, the F-4Ds deployed to Vahdati remained on

Top
These two early-delivery F-4Es, and their pilots, were photographed at Mehrabad air base in 1971. Iranian Phantom II crews were then receiving their training in the USA (*authors' collection*)

Above
An F-4E taxies in at Mehrabad air base in the mid-1970s, passing a C-130 on its way back to dispersal. Early Iranian E-models were built to Block 46 and 47 standards, and they were later equipped with wing leading-edge slats and Mod 556 cockpit upgrades (*authors' collection*)

This photograph of F-4E 75-0250 was taken shortly after its delivery to Iran, but prior to its assignment to a unit. The jet therefore lacks Iranian serials and a 'TFB number' (*US DoD*)

The first RF-4E built for Iran was 69-7590, seen here during a test flight in the US. The aircraft was rolled out of McDonnell Douglas's Phantom II factory in the autumn of 1970, and made its maiden flight on 14 December. Two reconnaissance RF-4s were already operational in Iran by then, however, the USAF having flown at least two RF-4Cs from bases in-country since early 1970. The first IIAF RF-4Es arrived in Iran on 3 March 1971, allowing both RF-4Cs to return to their base in Western Europe (*McDonnell Douglas/Boeing via the authors*)

the strength of the 306th TFW, operating under the command of Capt Reza Mohamad.

The third version of the Phantom II to be used by the IIAF/IRIAF remains the least-known – the photo-reconnaissance optimised RF-4E. Officially, only 16 newly-built aircraft were delivered between 1971 and 1979. They were equipped with some very advanced equipment, most of which was – during the early 1970s at least – under the constant control of USAF-personnel seconded to the IIAF. At the time, the USAF and the IIAF were involved in secret reconnaissance missions along Iran's borders with the USSR, seeking intelligence on radar stations and air bases.

These flights were generated to help Strategic Air Command probe the weak spots in Soviet radar coverage and air defences in order to find the most suitable points for launching deep penetration missions into Soviet territory in the event of war.

During one such flight, in November 1973, the IIAF suffered its first operational Phantom II loss when an RF-4E was rammed by a Soviet MiG-21. By 1978, at least two more RF-4Es, but probably three, had been lost – one certainly in 1977 over Yemen and another in a training incident. There are also indications that an additional jet came down during a reconnaissance flight over Soviet territory. Another photo-Phantom II suffered a badly damaged wing during a training flight in 1974-75.

By 1980, therefore, the IRIAF should have had only 11 or, at most, 12 RF-4Es in service. But that was not the case – there were actually between 19 and 21 reconnaissance Phantom IIs still in Iran! The reasons for this discrepancy were unofficial deliveries of 'white-tailed' RF-4Es, or possibly RF-4Cs, directly from the USAF. The Americans took great care to replace any Iranian Phantom IIs lost in operations from which both countries benefited, and at least six, and possibly as many as eight, RF-4Es, usually dubbed 'Unknown Iranians', had indeed been delivered to Iran by late 1978.

Like the Israeli Defence Forces Air Force (IDF/AF), the Iranians operated RF-4Es in flight strength within several different F-4E-equipped squadrons. During the 1970s and 1980s, RF-4Es were assigned to the 33rd TFS (usually four examples between 1971 and 1980), the 62nd TFS (up to eight

between 1973 and 1992) and the 61st TFS (usually four between 1974 and 1990). A few examples were also operated by the 11th TFW.

All Iranian Phantom II units were subordinated to Air Defence Command. This huge organisation also controlled four squadrons of F-14As and 12 of F-5A/B/E/Fs.

The F-4Es were mainly operated as fighter-bombers, armed with a full-range of US-supplied Mk 82, 83, 84 and M-117 general purpose (GP) bombs, plus AGM-65A Maverick electro-optic (TV) guided air-to-ground missiles. In addition, the F-4Ds could be equipped with AVQ-9 'Zot Box' cabin-mounted laser designators for use with the GBU-10 laser-guided bomb, which was based on the Mk 84 weapon. Both D- and E-models could also be equipped with British-supplied Hunting BL 755 cluster-bomb units (CBUs), as well as ALQ-71, -72 and -87 ECM (Electronic Counter-Measures) pods, about 80 of which were delivered to Iran by the USAF.

For interception, as well as self-defence, the F-4D/Es carried AIM-7E-2 and AIM-9J/P-1 air-to-air missiles, huge numbers of which had been purchased during the 1970s. These weapons were constantly upgraded through a series of modifications that were undertaken in the United States.

Unlike USAF RF-4Cs and IDF/AF RF-4Es and F-4E(S)s, Iranian RF-4Es could not be armed with Sidewinders. As a result, they relied exclusively on ECM pods and their speed for defence.

SUPPORT INFRASTRUCTURE

In 1980 the support infrastructure for the Iranian Phantom II fleet was still not complete. The priority during the 1970s had been to acquire the aircraft as soon as possible, and in the largest numbers. Facilities such as those needed for the complete overhaul and production of weapons (including AGM-65A Maverick missiles) were still to be fully developed, although Iranian

RF-4E 2-434 sits on the ramp at an undisclosed base in Iran in full IIAF colours and markings in the early 1970s. Iranian RF-4Es were fitted with the very latest USAF reconnaissance equipment prior to their delivery to Iran (authors' collection)

Iranian RF-4Es, and their crews, had already seen extensive service prior to the commencement of the Iran-Iraq War, flying many dangerous missions along – and sometimes beyond – the Soviet border, over Oman, Yemen and elsewhere. This example carries an ALQ-87(V)-3 ECM pod on the left inner underwing pylon (authors' collection)

Aircraft Industries (IACI), established next to Mehrabad International Airport in the mid-1970s by Northrop, was capable of completely overhauling and modifying F-4s by the time of the revolution.

And despite lacking the infrastructure required to fully service all aspects of the F-4, and its weapons systems, the Iranians could still muster huge quantities of spare parts, which had been purchased for its Phantom IIs during the 1970s. Indeed, the Shah declared that the armed forces as a whole must have enough spares to remain fully operational for six months of intensive war. This was achieved, but to maintain this stock level of parts, a complex computer-supported supply system called PeaceLog was installed by the Americans as well. During the revolution, however, PeaceLog fell apart when computer codes were lost and many huge depots were simply forgotten or their entrances sealed. The F-4E fleet was soon to suffer from the decentralisation of its maintenance structure.

The situation was different with the two F-4D-equipped units, however. Not only were their maintenance crews amongst the most experienced in the air force, they also had their spare parts store centralised on base. Consequently, the technicians from these two squadrons were able to maintain and support their own aircraft, and to help other units service and repair their F-4Es. This soon changed with the outbreak of war, for the F-4Ds of the 71st and 72nd FSs were dispersed in small detachments to several bases in southern and south-western Iran.

Sometime later, three badly-damaged F-4Ds were gathered at Mehrabad – where this version had hardly been seen since the early 1970s – to be used as a spares source. Although some reports suggest that these three aircraft never flew again, there are indications that at least one (and perhaps two) was completely rebuilt and returned to service some years after the war. By 1988, the remains of four F-4Ds which had either been shot down, crashed or destroyed on the ground during the war were gathered at Mehrabad for the recovery of spare parts.

Iranian F-4Es were often shifted around to different bases during the war. In the spring of 1981, for example, many from TFB 1 were sent to Vahdati to reinforce the permanent detachments from the 31st and 33rd TFWs that were based there for much of the war.

The technical condition of Iranian Phantom IIs initially remained good after the Islamic revolution, although continuous turmoil, strikes, protests, purges and forced retirements soon had their effect. Between March 1979 and September 1980, ten F-4s were lost and at least 16 crewmembers killed due primarily to technical problems attributed to poor maintenance.

Problems had beset the IIAF even before the revolution, with the whole air force having been virtually grounded in late 1978, bringing flying training almost to a halt. But from mid-1979 onwards, when there were signs of unrest in Iranian Kurdestan and Western Azerbaijan, some units were brought back into service, and they duly became involved in intensive combat activ-

F-4E 73-01551 was one of the last Phantom IIs delivered to Iran. Built to Block 57-59 standard, it was equipped with TISEO and could carry the AGM-65A Maverick air-to-ground-missile. The jet is seen here displaying the markings of the 61st TFW, stationed at Bushehr (TFB 6), during exercise *Nidlink '77* (*authors' collection*)

An ALQ-87(V)3 ECM pod-equipped Block 51-56 F-4E takes off from Mehrabad air base in the late 1970s. The aerials on the underside of the pod have been touched out on the photo by the IRIAF's official censor (*authors' collection*)

ity inside the own country. However, the overall effectiveness of the air force had not improved significantly by the summer of 1980.

In the meantime, the so-called 'Nojeh coup' – an attempt to overthrow the clerical regime by air force officers stationed at TFB 3 in June 1980 – had been exposed. More purges then took place, and some 300 officers (mainly pilots) were jailed. Most were executed. The result was a further deterioration in the air force's mission effectiveness, with restrictions on flying time and pilot training. Yet despite this, Iranian crews, and their Phantom IIs, were to survive this additional ordeal. But the personnel profile of IRIAF F-4 units was changing.

Most pilots who had joined the air force before 1977 had been trained in the United States or Pakistan. Some had even served on exchange postings with the USAF and IDF/AF, and a few were permitted to make clandestine test flights in MiGs at secret American establishments. The end result of all this was a cadre of highly skilled crews that were able to use their F-4s to their fullest extent, even if most lacked combat experience.

From 1977 onwards, however, the quality of aircrew training varied considerably. Cadets initially received training comparable to that offered to USAF or US Navy trainee crews, but from mid-1978 it deteriorated as the political situation in Iran began to change. Of those crews in training during the second half of 1978, hardly any completed the syllabus. Some were to become indoctrinated by the clergy and sent to combat units, where they served not only as pilots, but also as 'political commissars'.

Iranian F-4s were usually crewed by two pilots. Those in the front seat generally held the rank of captain or higher, while the second crewman was drawn from the lower ranks, being either second or first lieutenants fresh from training. Whilst under training, crew members would change places as the syllabus progressed so as to give junior pilots front seat expe-

A pristine F-4E of the 71st TFW departs Shiraz air base. Within weeks of the Iran-Iraq War commencing in September 1980, the 71st TFW replaced its F-4Es with F-4Ds. The wing's 71st and 72nd TFSs had prior experience on the D-model Phantom II, having operated F-4Ds in the mid-1970s (*authors' collection*)

rience – once war started, this often took place during actual combat missions. In some cases, personnel remained together for long periods, while in others, senior pilots were paired with junior crewmen. And in what Iranian Phantom II crews considered to be a 'worst case scenario', pilots flew with 'backseaters' that had earned their qualification more for their support for the new clerical regime, rather than for their

ability in the cockpit. In some cases, this loyalty was rewarded with promotion to high rank.

Throughout the conflict, there was much shifting of pilots and technical personnel between units, mainly to replace operational losses. But there were other, more sinister, reasons for these transfers. When war broke out in September 1980, many fast jet pilots were languishing in prison – although nothing like as

Streaming its braking parachute, a storeless F-4E from the 71st TFW rolls down the runway at Shiraz air base shortly after completing a peacetime training flight (*authors' collection*)

many as has been reported in the West. In some units there were more jets than crews to fly them, with pilot numbers being particularly low.

As a result of the Iraqi attack, Iranian President Bani-Sadr pardoned most jailed officers on 23 September 1980. Some were sent straight back to their units, while others were given several days' leave with their families and then sent on indoctrination courses to learn about the 'crimes of the Shah and his regime'. Most pilots released in October 1980 had previously been sentenced to death by the Khomeini regime, and today the survivors find it hard to comprehend that they were saved from certain death by the Iraqi invasion of Iran, which they were then sent to repel!

From the start of the war, many pilots were concentrated in the combat zone from units spread across Iran, and particularly from those based at TFBs 9 and 10. Squadrons on the same airfields frequently swapped aircraft, resulting in many pilots becoming proficient on several different types. Indeed, around 80 per cent of F-4 pilots also flew the F-5E/F and the F-14 Tomcat. By 1981 Lockheed C-130 and Fokker F 27 transport pilots had also qualified to fly fast jets. This policy effectively meant that many pilots – especially those in the F-14-equipped units – were able to fly all three of Iran's main combat types, thus alleviating any potential attrition replacement problems. Some army helicopter pilots were also later transferred to the air force and qualified on the F-4 and F-5.

In practice, such jet swapping could see a pilot who, for example, was officially assigned to the 41st TFW with F-5E/Fs, flying F-4Es with the co-located 31st or the 33rd TFWs at TFB 3. Equally, he could just as easily be flown by a transport aircraft to another base in order to fly operationally with a unit in another part of the country. It was hardly

The last F-4E to be officially delivered to Iran was 75-0257, which was issued to the 11th TFW at Mehrabad air base in late 1978 – just two months before the Islamic Revolution swept the Shah from power. 75-0257 is seen here undergoing post-assembly checks at McDonnell Douglas's St Louis, Missouri, plant (*authors' collection*)

surprising, therefore, that little affinity developed between pilots and units, their chief loyalty instead being to their country. Colourful personal aircraft markings were few, although pilots did wear type and squadron patches on their clothing.

LOYALTY UNDER SUSPICION

Pressure from the controlling regime compelled the IRIAF to concentrate those pilots whose loyalty was considered suspect, or who were thought likely to defect, at certain bases. Vahdati (TFB 4) was known to have a high proportion of the 'Shah's pilots', as they were dubbed. These men were kept under constant surveillance by commanding officers who supported the regime, or at least pretended to. After the failed Nojeh coup attempt, many promotions were frozen and some officers were downgraded in rank. Purges and forced retirements also led to the unusual situation where pilots with the rank of major were given command of tactical fighter wings, or even bases, and captains made COs of squadrons.

This was not an easy time to be an IRIAF officer, for distrust often lurked just beneath the surface of supposed friendship. But pilots who distinguished themselves in combat soon became respected, and in some cases achieved legendary status. Maj Daryush 'Z' (his full name cannot be revealed in order to protect his identity) was a veteran F-4 and F-5 pilot with 1500 hrs of combat experience achieved during the war with Iraq. His summation of the situation facing his fellow officers in the IRIAF is both stark and bitter;

'Under the political circumstances of the time, the IRIAF High Command had to develop its own mandates for combat pilots during the war, the most important of which frequently had nothing to do with the flying and combat performance of the pilots. These requirements changed as the war advanced, and were roughly as follows. At the start of the war, the number one requirement for the Iranian pilot was the right answer to the question, "Will you save us?", which was posed by the political leaders of the regime. In the weeks after the start of the war, it became; "Can we trust you?" Once the Iraqi push deep into Iran had been stopped, the number one requirement changed to, "Can we trust you, and do we need you?" After the war started to go badly for Iran once again, it changed to, "Can we trust you, and can you fly this mission?"

'From 1984-85, the IRIAF started to run out of spare parts, so the number one requirement changed to "Do we trust you, and can you fly the combat sortie in a less than fully serviceable fighter?" Finally, after eight years of war, the number one requirement for an Iranian fighter pilot became very simple – stay alive.'

Indeed, by the end of the war surviving pilots were completely exhausted, and most looked at least ten years older than they were. The condition of their Phantom IIs was not much better. Most had been badly damaged several times over and then been repaired, and the fleet was in need of a complete overhaul. No modifications had been carried out during the war, and it was only late on in the conflict that new weapons were introduced. Nevertheless, technical problems were solved one by one, and even today all three marks of the F-4 Phantom II continue to form the main fighter-bomber strength of the IRIAF.

IRAQ INVADES

It was to have been 1967 all over again – a lightning-fast strike to neutralise the enemy's air power on the ground. The tactic had been employed with brilliant success by the Israelis to give them a head-start in the Six Day War, and the Iraqis could see no reason why it should not succeed again.

Accordingly, at noon on 22 September 1980, Saddam Hussein's air force launched an attack on key Iranian bases. Two waves of fighter-bombers, one numbering no fewer than 192 aircraft and the other 60, struck eight key air bases, four other airfields and four army facilities in order to pave the way for a land thrust deep into Iran. But the attacks did not quite go to plan due to poor mission execution, an overall lack of target intelligence and the use of unsuitable weapons against huge hardened installations. As a result, the first surprise attack failed. Indeed, most of the jets parked in the open escaped destruction, with little more than superficial damage being inflicted. However, an F-4E at Mehrabad was cut in two forward of the air intakes in a rocket attack by three MiG-23s.

The outbreak of the Iran-Iraq War did not represent the first time that Iranian Phantom IIs had tasted combat, however. Six years earlier, in 1974-75, the IIAF had flown its F-4s in sorties against Marxist rebels in the Omani province of Dhofar. Months later, they had seen brief, but fierce, action against the Iraqis, with Iranian pilots scoring successes with AGM-65A Maverick missiles to the surprise of their American instructors and other Western observers. Shortly after the Islamic revolution in 1979, the IRIAF was compelled to use Phantom IIs

The first Iranian Phantom II destroyed by the Iraqis was hit on the ramp at Mehrabad shortly after 1400 hrs on 22 September 1980. The aircraft was practically cut in two by unguided rockets fired by three Iraqi MiG-23BNs (*authors' collection*)

Another photograph of the F-4E destroyed at Mehrabad. The aircraft was hit while parked outside the IACI facility, where it was awaiting refurbishment (*authors' collection*)

17

during fierce fighting against uprisings in Iranian Kurdistan and Western Azerbaijan. Finally, during the initial skirmishes with Iraq in August and September 1980 which preceded the main Iraqi attack, the IRIAF scored three or four aerial kills, but also suffered several losses to flak or SAMs.

The first action for the F-4 in the war with Iraq came just minutes after the MiG-23 attack on Mehrabad. As technicians rushed towards the damaged Phantom IIs, two F-4Es scrambled to intercept the departing Iraqi MiGs. What happened next is not entirely clear. It is known that the Iraqis dispatched six MiG-23s to attack Mehrabad, but that only three – led by an Iraqi major – reached their target. In fact the Iranians claimed five Iraqi aircraft downed from the west of Tehran to the Iraqi border in the minutes after the Mehrabad strike. At least one pilot, reported to have been an Egyptian, ejected from his MiG, but his fate remains unknown.

THE FIRST COUNTERATTACK

While other Iranian fighters were still occupied engaging the Iraqi attackers, or flying combat air patrols (CAP), the pilots and technicians at Shahrokhi/Nojeh (TFB 3) and Bushehr (TFB 6) were already preparing for the first retaliatory raids on Iraq. Initially, there had been confusion, but once it became known that Iraq was launching an invasion, the IRIAF began putting into effect contingency plans devised in peacetime.

Barely two hours after the first Iraqi strike, crews from the 31st, 32nd and 61st TFWs prepared for their first missions against Iraq. They targeted the most important air bases that could be reached by their F-4s, which included Rashid, south of Baghdad, and Shoaibah, near Basrah. In addition to being a training centre, Rashid was known to be home to single MiG-21MF, MiG-23MS and MiG-23BN squadrons.

The 31st TFW prepared four F-4Es, each armed with six Mk 82 bombs and two Sparrow missiles, while the leading aircraft in each pair also carried two Sidewinders and an ECM pod for the attack on Rashid. Taking off at around 1600 hrs, the Phantom IIs entered Iraqi airspace at high speed and very low level, taking the air defences completely by surprise. Not a single flak round was fired, nor any SAMs launched. Little opposition was encountered when the Phantom IIs reached Baghdad either, the weak response from air defence brigades of the Iraqi Air Force/Air Defence Command (IrAF/ADC) failing to stop the IIRAF from taking the war to the Iraqi capital. The F-4 crews successfully dropped their bombs on Rashid before escaping unscathed.

Minutes later a second formation of four Phantom IIs, led by Lt Col Sepidmooy-Azar, took-off from Bushehr. Flying as the leader's wingman was Capt Dejpassand, with Capt Alireza Yassini (and WSO Capt Massood Eqdam) in the No 3 spot and Capt Fe'li-Zadeh as No 4. All the F-4s were armed with Mk 83 bombs. Once airborne, the crews formed up and followed the coastline north, via Bandar-e Deilam and Qorveh, to Khosro-Abad, and then over the Shatt al-Arab waterway into Iraqi airspace. Their target was Shoaibah air base, which was then one of the IrAF's most important facilities.

IRAQI 'FOXBATS'

In 1977 the Iraqis had ordered more than 240 aircraft and 60 helicopters from the USSR. Amongst the fast jets supplied by the Soviet Union were

24 MiG-25 'Foxbats', which were sold to the IrAF under the following conditions: the aircraft would not be fitted with the latest Soviet avionics or weapons; the number of Russian advisers in Iraq would be increased from 6000 to 18,000 (at a time when the whole IrAF numbered only 14,000 personnel!); and the MiG-25 deployment to Iraq would be organised and conducted under strict Soviet control.

In early 1980, the Soviets despatched the first 14 MiG-25s to Shoaibah, escorted by 20 MiG-23s. Ten MiG-25R/PDs – in full Iraqi markings – followed, so that by mid-1980 a total of 24 MiG-25s were operational at Shoaibah. Despite Moscow's protests about the Iraqi invasion of Iran, and an official declaration of neutrality, Soviet advisers were still in-country when the Iraqis launched their attack in September 1980.

Officially the MiG-25s formed 'B Flight' of the IrAF's 1st Squadron, yet in reality a mere four MiG-25Rs were placed under the direct control of the Iraqi-manned 1st Reconnaissance-Strike Squadron.

As with the 'Foxbats', the newly-delivered MiG-23s were also flown by foreign pilots, usually Soviets or East Germans. Indeed, during the first skirmishes in August and September 1980, the Iranians had noticed that the Shoaibah MiG-23s were flown in a particularly aggressive manner.

Keen to neutralise the threat posed by the MiG-23 and MiG-25 units at Shoaibah, the IRIAF despatched their F-4s to attack this prized target late in the afternoon of 22 September 1980.

Leading his formation at very low level, Sepidmooy-Azar initially passed far to the south of the target, thundering over the Faw Peninsula and reaching Um Qassr, before turning north. There was no reaction from the Iraqi air defences. Obviously, they had not expected such a swift response, still less an attacking force to take such a circuitous route. The Iraqis were also confident that their own strike had been effective enough to prevent an IRIAF reaction for at least 48 hours, so their air defence system was not activated.

Despite the glare of the sun, the target was found with little difficulty. The formation split, Sepidmooy-Azar making a 360-degree turn to give the rest of his section time to deploy to the right and left of him, before resuming his original course. He then climbed to acquire the target, rolled out and dived to drop his bombs. Seconds later, Dejpassand and Yassini hit the target from the right and left. Fe'li-Zadeh was the last to attack, and did so from the same direction as Sepidmooy-Azar. Minutes later, all four Phantom IIs thundered away in an easterly direction, leaving Shoaibah wreathed in a huge cloud of smoke. There was still no resistance from the air defences.

The F-4's first combat mission from Bushehr had gone exactly as planned, and for the next few weeks the 'Iraqi' MiG-23s and MiG-25s did not reappear over Iran. In fact, they had been pulled back to al-Wallid air base (H-3) in western Iraq, near the Jordanian border. Maj Daryush 'Z' explained the tactics used during attacks such as this;

'During the first years of the war, when we attacked in larger numbers, our main tactic was to hit the target by flying low at high speeds, closing from all points of the compass. Each IRIAF fighter was more or less flying straight into the target and, in many cases, at each other. We relied on altitude and timing to avoid collisions as we crossed each other's flight paths. Over the target, it took great pilot discipline to use this tactic, but it proved successful. Crews were spaced so that between four and six aircraft – depending on the size of strike – could hit the target almost simultaneously. The Iraqi defenders had neither the time to get their flak guns fully traversed or their SAMs guiding correctly, nor did they know where the actual attack was coming from. They could not use the flightpath of the first Iranian aircraft over the target to predict that of the next, therefore reducing the chance of them locking onto a jet with computer-guided flak or a SAM.'

A further 50 combat sorties were flown by Phantom II crews from Bushehr, Nojeh and other bases in the dusk hours of 22 September 1980. Among the attacks was a devastating strike by two F-4Es on Um Qassr naval and air base in which Mk 117 GP bombs were launched at several small Iraqi naval vessels. In addition, two HY-2G 'Seersucker' missile sites that were threatening shipping in the northern Persian Gulf from their position on the banks of the Shatt al-Arab waterway were destroyed.

THE 140-FIGHTER RAID

Recovering from the shock of the Iraqi attack, the Iranians worked intensively during the night of 22-23 September to prepare as many aircraft for operations as possible. The IRIAF's intention for the following morning was to go all-out to pursue what it saw as its main objective – establishing air superiority over the battlefield by neutralising the IrAF. This was to be the main task for the next few days until the target list was both partially exhausted and partially changed.

While the technicians worked on the aircraft, armourers began the back-breaking job of loading the aircraft up with ordnance. Literally hundreds of Mk 82, 83 and 84 GP bombs, Hunting BL 755 CBUs, AGM-65A Maverick TV-guided air-to-surface missiles and AIM-7E Sparrow and AIM-9P-1 Sidewinder air-to-air missiles were retrieved from storage in the extensive underground ammunition magazines at each air base.

During the first few days of the Iran-Iraq War, the IRIAF flew intensive combat operations, focusing its force of F-4Es at Nojeh, Bushehr and Mehrabad. Units already based at these locations had their operational strength boosted through the transferring in of Phantom IIs from the 91st and 101st TFWs, based in eastern and southern Iran. This series of base shifts resulted in some 40 F-4s being concentrated at each of these airfields. This photograph shows a Phantom II being prepared for its impending move westward (authors' collection)

The damage inflicted upon Iran during the Iraqi invasion was massive. Indeed, no IRIAF pilot could ignore scenes like this – vessels sunk or destroyed by Iraqi artillery near Khoramshahr harbour (authors' collection)

During the war with Iraq the Iranian Phantom II fleet was supported by 14 Boeing 707-3J9C tankers, one of which (5-242) is seen here prior to its delivery to the IIAF at Boeing's Seattle plant in 1975 (*authors' collection*)

The Iranians also operated five Boeing 747-2J9C tankers and airborne command posts (such as 5-8701) in support of Phantom II strikes deep into Iraq (*authors' collection*)

This pilot's map shows the Baghdad area of operations. Of special interest is a ring of airfields built around – and even inside – the city, as well as the hilly areas along the international border (upper right corner), which Iranian F-4 pilots used to penetrate deep into Iraq without being detected by air defences (*NIMA Tactical Pilotage Chart, 1:500,000 scale*)

Having considered existing plans, and hastily adapted them to the current situation facing the IRIAF shortly before dawn on the war's second day, the air force's High Command issued an air tasking order to three of its main bases, Bushehr, Nojeh and Mehrabad. Minutes later, Col Dadpay, Bushehr's commanding officer, entered the ready room in which pilots of the 61st TFW had already gathered. Dadpay opened his briefing with the remark;

'In response to the Iraqi invasion of Iran, it has been decided that today we will attack all Iraqi air bases with a force in excess of 140 combat aircraft. From our base, 40 Phantom IIs have been allocated to the plan.'

A similar number of F-4s would take off from Mehrabad and Nojeh.

The biggest problem with such a massive operation was the IRIAF's lack of suitable tanker aircraft. It possessed just 14 Boeing 707-3J9Cs and four Boeing 747-2J9C tankers, and these would be unable to refuel all the strike aircraft en route to the target. This meant that many of the Phantom IIs from Nojeh, which were to leave first to attack targets near Baghdad, would have to conduct their sorties without in-flight refuelling. Those from Mehrabad would follow two minutes later, but they would be refuelled. Two minutes behind them, the 61st TFW would start launching its aircraft, and they would also rendezvous with tankers over the border. In addition to the 120 Phantom IIs, 20 F-5E/F Tiger IIs from two forward air bases (TFB 2, near Tabriz, and TFB 4 Vahdati, near Dezful) would also participate in this operation.

Bushehr air base had never witnessed such a large-scale operation before. One after another, 40 F-4Es rolled out of their hardened aircraft shelters, while groundcrews made the final checks on ammunition and fuses, pulling safety pins to arm bombs and missiles. The aircraft taxied out to take off, while the local GCI (ground-controlled intercept) station started organising the formations, providing them with the necessary vectors to enable them to rendezvous with the tankers circling at 40,000 ft near the Iraqi border. After refuelling, each formation lost

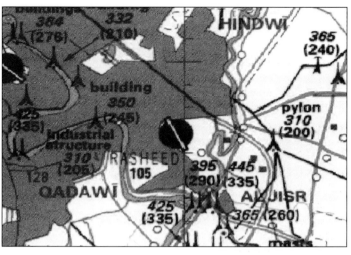

height in order to penetrate Iraqi airspace at very low level, with one formation from each of the bases converging on a target.

Although the US government had sold a vast array of modern weaponry to the Shah in the 1970s, it had refused to supply AGM-45A Shrike anti-radar missiles (ARMs), which meant that the IRIAF lacked an effective SEAD (suppression of enemy air defences) capability. Therefore, the only attack profile open to IRIAF crews in order to avoid being detected by radar-guided SAMs was to fly low, using terrain to mask their approach.

The objectives of this first massive strike were the Vasseliyah oil installations, two army barracks and a number of air bases. The latter included al-Rashid and al-Dadjil (near Baghdad), al-Hurriya (near Kirkuk), Mousel, Shoaibah and Tallil (all brand-new, near Nasseriyah), al-Bakr (north of Baghdad) and Kut. Despite the simultaneous arrival of so many aircraft, disciplined flying at very low level achieved complete surprise – again, there was no reaction from the air defences.

Eight F-4Es from TFB 1, each toting six Mk 82s and four BL 755s, together with two Sparrows and three external fuel tanks, were scheduled to attack Rashid. They were accompanied by an RF-4E to take post-strike

An air navigation map of Baghdad, showing Rashid (spelt 'Rasheed' on the map) air base in the city's south-eastern suburbs, not far from the Tigris River. Note the high-rise buildings – Iranian F-4 pilots had to contend with enemy air defences and consider all possible obstacles when planning operations in this part of Iraq, which were usually flown at low level (*NIMA Tactical Pilotage Chart, 1:500,000 scale*)

This more detailed Russian map reveals details of Rashid air base. The two runways and long taxiway can clearly be seen, as can the nearby civilian areas. The airfield was attacked at least 15 times during the war's first month, leaving it extensively damaged. IRIAF pilots went to great lengths to ensure that civilian casualties were kept to a minimum (*authors' collection*)

photographs. Even before the mission had started, the crews were fully aware that they would be up against it in respect to fuel. The formation had been briefed to arrive and depart at the highest possible speed, but as there were only enough tankers to refuel the aircraft on their outward journey, nobody knew if they would be able to complete the mission. The aircraft left Mehrabad at 0530 hrs and, to reduce weight, the centreline drop tanks were left empty, only to be filled when the aircraft met the tankers over the border.

The eight F-4Es entered Iraqi airspace at low level in two four-ship formations, with the single RF-4E following further back. Over Baghdad, they were greeted by heavy, but inaccurate, anti-aircraft fire. Reaching the target, the Phantom II crews again executed their now familiar splitting manoeuvres and dropped their bombs, closing simultaneously from several different directions. Rashid was heavily hit, with several buildings being demolished, the runway cut in several places and many vehicles destroyed.

A Boeing 707-3J9C refuels two RF-4Es and two F-4Es. Tanker support was essential for Iranian pilots who had to rely on high speed and very low-level flight to penetrate deep into Iraq. The IRIAF tanker fleet was too small to support all sorties, and some crews often found themselves critically short of fuel when leaving Iraq (*authors' collection*)

This was the first time the IRIAF had undertaken such a large-scale operation, and with most pilots lacking combat experience, it was inevitable that mistakes in co-ordination would occur. One such error saw the first formation of eight F-4Es from Bushehr arrive over the Baghdad target area at low level just seconds after the Mehrabad Phantom IIs had started their attack. What followed echoed the experiences of bomber crews from World War 2, as several crews from the TFB 6 formation noticed bombs falling from above. Some initially thought that the IDF/AF was bombing Baghdad, although they soon realised that the bombs were coming from other IRIAF Phantom IIs releasing their ordnance from a higher altitude. Radio channels were quickly buzzing with warning calls, and by literally flying between Baghdad's high-rise buildings and then pulling up, the Bushehr F-4s evaded all the 'friendly' bombs, and resulting explosions, before making their own attacks.

Once back at Bushehr, the crews found that ten Nojeh aircraft had been forced to declare a fuel emergency and divert there, while several TFB 6 Phantom IIs which had been attacking targets further north were forced to land at Nojeh and even Mehrabad. Indeed, most of the crews who attacked targets in the Baghdad area experienced a shortage of fuel on their return to Iran.

In this pre-strike reconnaissance photograph of Rashid air base, two Hunters and a MiG-21 can be seen in the top right corner, as well as a MiG-23BN in the bottom corner. Note the low altitude at which this photograph was taken – it took bold Iranian pilots to fly these missions and bring back such images from one of the world's best defended cities (*authors' collection*)

The attacks cost the IRIAF three Phantom IIs, at least two of which were F-4Es, with the loss of four crewmembers. One F-4E crashed on take-off from Nojeh, killing Capt Khodabakhsh Eshqipour and 1Lt Abbas Eslami-Niya, who had chosen to stay in their crippled jet in order to avoid it hitting a nearby residential area.

TARGET OF OPPORTUNITY

After the success of the massive 140-aircraft strike, the IRIAF planned a repeat performance for the next day.

Capt Farassyabi was an RF-4E navigator based at TFB 1 during the war, and he participated in some of the most hazardous missions of the conflict. These would typically involve 30- to 40-minute flights over heavily defended areas. Farassyabi is seen here with an RF-4E pre-war (*authors' collection*)

Iranian RF-4E crews often experienced some particularly close calls. In this case, an Iraqi SA-2 missile passes within 300 ft of a Phantom II. During the early days of the war Iranian RF-4Es frequently operated in pairs, although combat attrition soon curtailed this practice. The longer the war lasted, the lonelier were the RF-4E crews' operations (*authors' collection*)

Once again, at 0530 hrs huge formations of Phantom IIs took off from Mehrabad, Nojeh and Bushehr to strike targets near Basrah, Baghdad and Mousel. Oil installations were also to be bombed. The first strike, by two F-4Es from Bushehr, hit the Zubair petrochemical complex near Basrah at precisely 0600 hrs, just as the morning shift was beginning. No less than 12 Mk 82 bombs were dropped on the complex, causing a series of volcanic explosions and creating tremendous fires which were to burn for more than a week. Zubair was reduced to ruins, with several square miles of burned out and twisted metal piping. At least 20 Iraqi and foreign technicians were killed in the raid.

Attacks like these represented a turning point in the war. Although Abadan refinery had come under Iraqi artillery fire, both sides had so far refrained from attacking each other's vulnerable oil installations. However, that same afternoon the IrAF retaliated with a strike on Iranian oil installations on Khark Island.

Aside from the strike on Zubair, the morning of 24 September saw Phantom IIs attack a series of Iraqi air bases, including al-Hurriya, on the outskirts of Kirkuk. This particular raid was performed by four F-4Es from Nojeh, led by Capt Abbas Dowran. One of the pilots on this mission was Capt H Assefi, who remembers;

'Prior to the mission being flown, Capt Dowran returned to TFB 3 from a secret gathering that was held on 23 September in Kerman province, where military commanders, senior clerics and government officials had discussed security and defence issues. Dowran in turn made it known to us that the war was now in full swing. Iran's rulers stressed the importance of a non-stop aerial campaign to be started, and maintained, against Iraqi forces at all cost, regardless of the loss of life. The intention was to hold the Iraqis back until the Basij (militia) and the Revolutionary Guard could be mobilised and brought to bear against the Iraqi forces. The government also ordered factories at Mashhad, Esfahan, Karaj, Semnan, Shiraz, Pairzan and Seman to be defended.

'Aircraft from TFB 3 had been in action against the Iraqis since the 22nd, and Capt Dowran now had new missions planned to take the fight to the enemy. The IrAF had opened the war with an initial attack on our air bases. These had destroyed only a few transport aeroplanes, although the Iraqis had hit our fuel stocks hard – so hard in fact that we had to order fuel for our air force from the USSR, which the Soviets flew in on aeroplanes that had been carrying MiG spares to Iraq just days earlier! Now Capt Dowran was making plans to target Iraqi fuel supplies. His plan called for four F-4Es from TFB 3 to hit one of Iraq's largest fuel storage areas some three kilometres west of al-Hurriya air base, near Kirkuk. At the same time, four F-4s from the 32nd TFS – operating from TFB 2 for this mission – would attack the Arbil fuel dump.

'Capt Dowran led our formation into Iraq. I flew as his wingman (with Lt R Emrouz as my WSO), with two other Phantom IIs following us. The leader's jet was armed with four BL 755 CBUs, two AIM-9s and two AIM-7 missiles, while the remaining three F-4s carried six Mk 82 bombs and four AIM-7 Sparrow missiles apiece. We planned for our Mk 82-equipped Phantom IIs to drop their bombs on the fuel storage area in a line abreast formation in a single wave, prior to departing the area. Capt Dowran would then swing over al-Hurriya to pay the Iraqis a visit.

'The fuel depot was larger than we had expected, and had been fairly well concealed by the Iraqis. There were no SAM sites, but many heavy flak guns. However, we flew in so low that of all the Iraqi 23 mm, 57 mm and 85 mm guns located at the depot, only the small calibre 23 mm weapons gave us reason to fear. As planned, we dropped our bombs on the depot and, detecting no MiGs in the area, we turned back towards Iran. We searched the sky for Capt Dowran's Phantom II, but all we could see was thick black smoke pouring from the now burning Iraqi fuel depot.

'Capt Dowran pulled up over al-Hurriya unopposed on his one-aeroplane raid. He had detected two MiG-21s just north of the enemy airfield, but he planned an exit before they had time to turn back. Dowran's F-4 picked up speed as he dropped his CBUs on the ramps in an effort to shut them down until they could be cleared by Iraqi engineers. Such a pass would also prevent any MiGs from being scrambled to intercept us.

'The captain's WSO spotted three Iraqi tank-carrying trucks near a hardened aircraft shelter, and Dowran could not help but take them out with his 20 mm gun during his last strafing run – his gun camera film later proved most entertaining, clearly showing his skill as a combat pilot. To our great relief, Capt Dowran soon rejoined our flight from astern, and we allowed him to lead us home.'

THE RAID FROM TFB 6

At noon on 24 September, TFB 6 again sortied another formation to attack Iraqi targets, this time near Kut. Two crews were selected for this mission – Col Mohagheghi was to lead (call sign 'Shahin-1'), with 1Lt Khosravi as his WSO, and Capt Alireza Yassini flew as his wingman ('Shahin-2'), with Capt Massood Eqdam in the rear cockpit. A further pair of Phantom IIs completed the formation, trailing the lead jets by several miles. For this mission each aircraft carried a hefty load of 12 Mk 82 Snakeye 500-lb retard bombs.

With the jets armed and fuelled and the crews thoroughly briefed, only a poor weather forecast of rain and heavy cloud cast doubt on the outcome of the raid.

After checking their aircraft inside the hardened shelters, the crews climbed into their cockpits to make their pre-flight checks. The auxiliary power units then came up to start the engines. Once their jets were fired up, the pilots signalled for the power units to be stopped and the aircrafts' on-board generators came on line. After satisfying themselves that everything was in working order, the crews rolled out of their hardened shelters and taxied to the end of the runway. Receiving clearance to take-off, they thundered into the sky on full afterburner. By the time Mohagheghi and Yassini were in the air, both aircraft in the second strike pair had developed technical problems, forcing their crews to abort the mission. Mohagheghi and Yassini pressed on regardless.

The flight plan called for the Phantom IIs to head for Abadan and Khoramshahr, before turning south and flying at low level over the northern tip of the Persian Gulf to Bubiyan Island, in Kuwait. They would then track along the Kuwaiti-Iraqi border, flying over uninhabited desert. This route should have allowed them to enter enemy airspace via the 'back door', thus once again taking Iraqi air defences by surprise. But this did not happen, for as the jets overflew Abadan, Mohagheghi and Eqdam spotted some 20 to 30 Iraqi tanks and artillery pieces being dug in opposite the Abadan oil refinery – then the world's largest – along the bank of the Shatt al-Arab. It was clear the Iraqis were planning to shell the refinery.

It was actually Eqdam who saw the Iraqi tanks first, the WSO calling over the intercom, 'Reza, they are targeting the Abadan refinery. What should we do?' Yassini immediately contacted the mission leader for a targeting change. '"Shahin-1", this is "Shahin-2". Several artillery pieces and tanks are behind sand mounds, targeting the Abadan refinery. Request diversion from the mission.' In response, came the instruction, 'Request granted, make a turn and hit them! We will go after the primary target'.

By chance, the Phantom II's flight path was such that the crew could easily see the raised gun barrels as they passed overhead. It was 1230 hrs, and the Iraqi troops were lining up for lunch. Seeing the bomb-laden F-4, they all hit the ground, but the Phantom II thundered harmlessly over them. Yassini had chosen to make a turn over Um Qassr and return to attack from the opposite direction. Intent on achieving total surprise, he flew at a height of barely ten feet over the flat, marshy terrain of the Faw Peninsula.

Closing on the target area, Yassini set his gun for the highest rate of fire. Lining up, he pumped 640 rounds from his fighter's 20 mm cannon into the Iraqi position, literally blowing several vehicles apart. Yassini pulled up to re-position his aircraft for a second pass, arming his bombs as he pushed over into a diving attack. His initial strafing run, followed by the 12 Mk 82 bombs, had given the Iraqis little chance to defend themselves, and not a single round was fired at Yassini's Phantom II prior to it departing south.

Little defensive fire was encountered by the 40 Phantom IIs sortied from Nojeh and Mehrabad either, these aircraft attacking targets inside Iraq – fuel depots near Faw, along with two nearby pumping stations. The Iraqi air defences had been effectively swamped by these attacks, the IrAF's radar network failing to detect the incoming Iranians in time to allow fighters to be scrambled or SAM sites to activate their missiles.

This Iraqi reconnaissance photograph reveals the sheer size of the Abadan oil refinery, which was then the world's largest. It came under fierce Iraqi artillery and air attack during the first days of the war and was severely damaged. Iraqi artillery positions attacked by the Phantom II flown by Capt Alireza Yassini and Capt Massood Eqdam on 24 September 1980 were sited on the other side of the Shatt al-Arab waterway, which can be seen in the background (*authors' collection*)

The IRIAF's counter-attacks continued into the morning of 25 September, with TFBs 1 and 3 launching two strikes against Tahmmouz (formerly Habbaniyah) and al-Taqqadum air bases. The targets lay very close together, some 74 kilometres west of Baghdad near Lake Habbaniyah. One of the pilots on the raid was Maj Kazem 'N', who takes up the story;

'Our strike force comprised eight Phantom IIs loaded with BL 755s and Mk 82s. Two jets were also armed with Sidewinders and Sparrows. We were briefed to follow the first formation of five F-4Ds and three F-4Es, which were to attack the target ten minutes before us. All the Phantom IIs were drawn from the 32nd and 33rd TFSs. Our headquarters hoped to surprise the Iraqis with a second strike so soon after the first. Al-Taqqadum was a large base, boasting two lengthy runways, a huge fuel dump and virtually the entire IrAF bomber fleet, which we specifically targeted.

'Our attack went as planned. Once over al-Taqqadum, we saw no Iraqi fighters in the air, and only a solitary F-4D had been hit by flak over the target – despite the damage, the jet appeared to be capable of making it back to Iran. The F-4Ds were the fastest aeroplanes in the IRIAF, but this flak-damaged jet was now the slowest F-4 ever! The mission leader ordered the two F-4Es armed with air-to-air missiles to stay with the damaged Phantom II and nurse it back to Iran. We were ordered to depart for the border.

'Later, I was told what happened. As the F-4D moved slowly towards the tanker, the escorting F-4Es, employing their "Combat Tree" equipment, detected four MiG-21s about 55 kilometres away – the IrAF fighters had been spotted soon after they had taken off from Kirkuk. They were planning on sneaking up on the trio of Phantom IIs as they neared the Iranian border. The leader of the F-4Es turned into the threat to take the

27

initiative away from the Iraqis, as he had been taught in training. The Iraqis must have then been alerted, for as the Phantom IIs closed on the MiGs, they broke off in pairs. This did not stop the F-4E wingman from firing a single Sparrow at the nearest MiG. The missile missed its mark and both Phantom II crews switched to Sidewinders as they closed to within three kilometres of the Iraqi fighters.

'Another MiG-21 then cut across their flight path, and the Phantom IIs broke hard left in an effort to follow them – thus flying into a well-laid trap. Barely a minute later, the F-4E wingman called out a missile warning and then broke away, trying to draw off a MiG that had worked his way behind them. But two R-13 Atoll missiles were already in the air, one of which flew into the ground. The second hit the right engine of the lead Phantom II, however. Although the warhead had failed to explode, the missile had knocked out the jet's afterburner. The crew had barely felt the Atoll hit, but the damage meant that the afterburner could not be engaged for fear of causing more damage to the F-4. The tailfin was also damaged, and the aircraft would no longer fly straight.

'The F-4E wingman had, in the meantime, got behind one of the MiGs and shot it down with a single Sidewinder. But the Iraqis were not withdrawing. As the lead Phantom II called for his wingman to check his damaged tail, another MiG closed on the IRIAF fighters at high speed from the left, firing his gun. A 23 mm round hit the cockpit just behind the windscreen and exploded, badly injuring the pilot's left hand and foot. The F-4E's APQ-120 radar and weapons control system, as well as the radio and intercom, were also knocked out. Cool air began blowing into the cockpit, but fortunately there was no fire and the pilot maintained control.

The wingman chased the MiG away and then returned to the two damaged Phantom IIs, leading them back home. Both landed at Qassr-e Shirin just as the base came under Iraqi air attack. The aircraft were quickly dragged into a hardened shelter so that their crews could be released and the injured pilot taken to hospital – he lost two-thirds of his left foot and three fingers from his left hand, leaving him unfit to fly the Phantom II.'

The attacks on Tammouz and al-Taqqadum were successful, Iranian pilots claiming nine aircraft destroyed on the ground and both runways at al-Taqqadum disabled in three different spots. Furthermore, the raid diverted the attention of the air defences from the following formations, which were to attack from the north. At 0500 hrs, two strikes penetrated Iraqi airspace at low level and bombed al-Hurriya air base, near Kirkuk, where at least one Antonov An-24TV was destroyed and a MiG-21

Written off by Western observers, the Iranian F-14A fleet also flew intensive combat operations right from the start of the war. The strike against Iraqi airfields in the Baghdad area on 25 September 1980 was covered by at least two pairs of Tomcats, which in turn shot down two Iraqi MiG-23s while protecting the departing Phantom IIs (*authors' collection*)

25 September 1980 also saw Phantom IIs from TFB 3 successfully attacked al-Hurriya AB, near Kirkuk. Several Iraqi aircraft were destroyed on the ground, including an Antonov An-24TV. Note the traces of fuel and fire-extinguishing foam near a MiG-21MF which was also damaged during the strike (*authors' collection*)

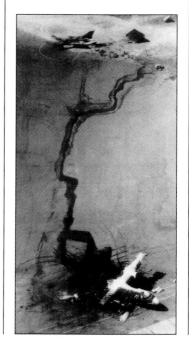

damaged on the ground. At Qayyarah air base, several hardened shelters were hit and aircraft destroyed.

CUTTING THE OIL PIPELINE

More F-4Es and F-5E/Fs subsequently targeted Iraqi oil installations in the area, hitting several refineries and causing so much damage that oil exports via the pipeline through Turkey were effectively cut. Just minutes later, the next Iranian Phantom II section flew to the north of Baghdad, then turned south and closed on the capital's airport, flying just above the Tigris River. Again total surprise was achieved. The crews dropped their bombs undisturbed, the last two sections attacking the Rashid base complex south of Baghdad. Col 'K G', then a junior pilot stationed at Mehrabad, remembers that mission;

'At 2200 hrs on the night before the attack, the IRIAF's higher command assigned 18 pilots for this important mission to Rashid. Nine Phantom IIs were committed – eight F-4Es armed with bombs and missiles, and an RF-4E for post-strike reconnaissance of the target. The only problem was fuel. Nobody knew if there would be enough to fulfil the mission. Pilots were briefed to refuel over Kermanshah on their way to the target, but were not told where to land after the mission. Finally, after working on mission planning deep into the night, the decision was made to land at Hamedan or Tehran, or anywhere else on the way. It was my first combat mission. I had not even seen a live bomb.

'The night before, looking under my F-4, I was horrified to see six bombs, two missiles, an ECM pod and three external fuel tanks. To avoid increasing weight beyond the permitted level, the central external tank was left empty to be filled later by the tanker. My pilot on that mission was Capt Daryush Yazdanfar, who although relatively inexperienced, insisted that we should hit the target, even if it cost us our own lives.

'At about 0530 hrs the jets took off from Mehrabad as two four-ship flights, with the single RF-4E flying behind us. We refuelled over Kermanshah one by one. While refuelling we were fired at, and the shooting continued along the border. Nevertheless, we entered Iraq while the RF-4 lagged behind to take post-strike pictures. I was a part of the first flight.

'Once inside, we continued to attract heavy anti-aircraft fire. Near the target, I asked the pilot to check the fuel. He said he did not know how to use the central fuel tank, and neither did I! However, we pressed on, knowing that this fuel would not help us reach the border on our return. Our fuel state also meant that we were not allowed to fly over the target more than once. We had to hit our targets on the first pass and leave. And although we had aimed a little short of the target during the actual strike, parts of the runway, the tarmac and the installations were hit. I glanced at the targeted area and saw a building collapsing and a trailer being blown up by the force of the explosions.

Post-strike reconnaissance photographs showed the results of the al-Hurriya strike on 25 September. Note the smoke from the bomb crater directly on top of the hardened aircraft shelter – evidence of the Iranian Phantom II pilots' aim – although the bomb failed to penetrate and only cracked the structure. The two MiG-21MFs seem to have survived the attack undamaged, having been pulled out of the damaged shelter (*authors' collection*)

'We departed Baghdad safely. Again, I asked about the fuel status. Yazdanfar replied "About 4000 lbs". It was not enough to reach the border. I told him to drop the external tanks in order to lower our weight and fuel consumption, while increasing speed. His inexperience in this procedure meant that we nearly hit the ground, for when the tanks were jettisoned the aircraft's nose pitched up, making control difficult.

'By then the sun was coming up. We didn't know how many of our aircraft were safe – we could see only two jets flying ahead of us. At first I thought they were Iraqis, but we later identified them as our own F-4s.

'We followed them to the border, intending to land at one of our bases. Looking out to our left, I saw four more Phantom IIs, with others flying behind then. Suddenly, I saw F-4s all around, but at lower altitudes, flying towards Iran. We crossed the border, and in order to conserve fuel, all jets gained altitude, and we duly followed suit, However, our fuel level had by then dropped to only 900 lbs at 14,000 ft – too low. With less than 1500 lbs of fuel aboard, there is a very high danger of the F-4's J79 engines flaming out. We were in the middle of nowhere, with only 900 lbs of fuel left. We knew we were over the Iranian mountains, but not exactly where. I was terrified, and yelled several times over the radio, "We're running out of fuel. Help us! Does anybody have us on radar?"

'There was no answer. Then I saw the Kermanshah army aviation base and told Yazdanfar to land there on its unfamiliar runway. We knew there was no facility for jets at Kermanshah, and that it was too short for the F-4 to land safely. With just 400 lbs of fuel left we had no choice. Expecting the engines to flame out at any moment, we lowered the landing gear and suddenly the jet started to yaw to the left. Yazdanfar shouted, "We've been hit. We cannot land with flaps". It meant that our approach speed would be 20 knots higher than normal, and considerably more braking would be needed to stop the jet. And of course the runway was not long enough either.

'We approached with difficulty, but suddenly to our disbelief we saw a jet sat in the middle of the runway, stuck in a bomb crater with a burst tyre. In the little time available we decided to pass over the stricken aeroplane and land beyond it, as we had no fuel left to overshoot and try again. We did not have time to think about landing a jet at 200 knots on such a short runway. Yazdanfar said, "We should eject!", but I replied, "No! We must land the aircraft in one piece, for at least its airframe will be of some use".

'At this very moment something unexpected happened. Another F-4 landed on the other side of the runway, apparently out of fuel too. Its pilot somehow managed to stop on the short runway, and when he saw us pass overhead, he rapidly cleared the runway for us. I asked Yazdanfar for the fuel status – "200 lbs". He pulled the Phantom II up and decided to make a fast turn and then land. He tried to turn as fast as possible and align the jet with the

After successfully bombing targets in the Baghdad area on 25 September 1980, Capt Daryush Yazdanfar and Lt 'K G' returned to Iran literally on fuel vapours. After two attempts to land on the short runway at the Iranian army air base near Kermanshah, they ran out of fuel and had to eject moments after touching down. Their F-4E survived because it landed on soft ground, allowing the empty drop tanks to cushion the impact. After repairs, the aircraft was able to fly many more combat sorties against the Iraqis (*authors' collection*)

runway, but his speed was too high. I yelled that it was too high, and he answered that the fuel had run out.

'When we finally touched down on the runway threshold, the F-4 bounced back into the air because of our excessive speed. We both shoved our respective control columns forward to lower the nose and the jet finally settled on the runway. We then engaged the brakes, but the fighter did not stop. Peering out of the cockpit, I saw a second Phantom II stuck in the middle of the runway, with two bombs still hanging under its wings. We were barely a second from colliding with it when Yazdanfar pulled off the runway. We still had 110 knots of speed when I saw a large hole ahead of us, right in our path. At that moment the canopies were jettisoned and I felt a pain in my waist. We both ejected.

'Landing at last, I looked across at our F-4, which had stopped on the soft ground almost intact, and had not caught fire because of its empty tanks. The external tanks had been crushed in the impact and absorbed its force. Moments later a rescue helicopter arrived and took us to hospital.'

'BRIDGE BUSTING'

After targeting Iraqi air bases in the war's opening days, the IRIAF now broadened its missions. The war was only four days old when at 1400 hrs on 26 September three F-4Es from TFB 6 were briefed to attack a strategic supply bridge east of Basrah. Five of the chosen crewmen were Capts Sadjedi, Hossein Nazari, Jalal Damiriyan and Alireza Yassini and Lt Ranjbar. They were specifically selected because they had been trained for 'bridge busting' missions. As always, the pilots and their commanders picked main and secondary targets, the idea being that if the main target was effectively destroyed, the other members of the formation would be free to attack the secondary ones. However, lack of up-to-date intelligence early on in the war often precluded effective selection of targets, leaving pilots to search for suitable targets of opportunity themselves.

The formation crossed the Shatt al-Arab then arrived over Basrah, slowing down to find the target. When it was finally in sight, the lead F-4, flown by Yassini, climbed slightly and then went into a shallow dive to enable the WSO to acquire the bridge and fire two Mavericks at it. Both missiles scored direct hits and the bridge was completely obliterated.

The second phase of the mission opened with the rest of the formation seeking targets of opportunity. The No 2 F-4, flown by Sadjedi, found and destroyed two Iraqi tanks, while Nazari sighted a large merchant ship in the port of Basrah. He made a tight turn to enable his WSO, Ranjbar, to establish a full lock-on and fire a single Maverick. As Nazari made a second turn, another AGM-65 was launched. Both missiles found their mark, a series of explosions wrecking the ship. Fires, and a huge column of smoke, could be seen from beyond the border. Iranian intelligence later learned that the vessel had been unloading military supplies when it was attacked.

Only seconds away from starting its take-off run, this F-4E from the 61st TFW is armed with four AGM-65A Maverick missiles. During the early days of the war the IRIAF suffered from a shortage of AGM-65-qualified Phantom II crews, resulting in numerous pilots and WSOs having to be trained during actual combat sorties (*authors' collection*)

IRAN COUNTERATTACKS

By late September 1980, the IRIAF had exhausted its main target list. Most Iraqi air bases – except those in the west of the country – had been heavily hit by repeated strikes. The IrAF responded by sending transport and bomber aircraft, as well as most of its reserve fighters and other high value assets to its western bases, and even to Jordan and Saudi Arabia. And with the Iraqis now also targeting the Iranian oil industry, the IRIAF changed its strategy from all out base attacks to an interdiction campaign, which was to last for the rest of the war.

On 30 September at 0530 hrs, several Phantom II formations penetrated Iraqi airspace. Four jets, armed with six Mk 82 bombs and carrying ALQ-87(V)-3 ECM pods, successfully flew through a corridor in the SAM belt between Salman Pak and Baghdad without being detected. Two of them targeted the site of the 'Tammouz' nuclear reactor in Tuwaitha, a southern suburb of Baghdad. Contrary to reports, the bombs did not miss the $275 m reactor core, but were specifically aimed at secondary installations. The result was the destruction of important research facilities, a large fire and casualties, as well as panic among French technicians working there. At the time the Iranians were not sure if the reactor was filled, and they wanted to avoid nuclear fall-out.

Five minutes later two further formations of F-4s appeared over Arbil and Neinava, where they hit local oil facilities and refineries. Although at least one of the Iranian sections involved was intercepted by two Iraqi MiG-23MSs during its retreat, the Phantom IIs successfully avoided the missiles fired at them and escaped unscathed. The IRIAF also flew numerous battlefield air interdiction (BAI) missions, striking targets immediately behind the frontline and causing considerable damage. For example, that morning two F-4Es destroyed an Iraqi ammunition dump 12 miles west of Ahwaz. Most BAI sorties were pre-planned, but some were simply opportunistic armed reconnaissance flights.

In the *New York Times* of 3 October, an American reporter described an F-4E passing barely 100 ft over his taxi, which was travelling along the Iraqi side of the Shatt al-Arab. He reported that the Phantom II

IRIAF armourers mount a TER (Triple Ejector Rack), with pre-loaded Mk 82 Snakeyes, onto an F-4E parked inside a hardened shelter. Thanks to the work of the Iranian technicians and armourers, the number of bombs which failed to explode was surprisingly low. Note also the strike-camera housing under the wing leading edge fuselage joint. Late-build Iranian F-4Es were equipped with cameras in the USA, this equipment enabling film to be used not only for bomb damage assessment, but also for intelligence gathering (*authors' collection*)

had turned and attempted to attack the vehicle. If nothing else, this story shows the freedom of operation enjoyed by the IRIAF, and in particular the Phantom IIs, which could move freely over the front as their APX-80 'Combat Tree' IFF enabled them to detect Iraqi fighters well in advance.

Following a short break due to adverse weather, 30 Phantom IIs attacked eight different Iraqi targets mainly in the Basrah area at 0530 hrs on 3 October. All four airfields near the southern city were hit, as were two deep-sea oil terminals near the port of Faw. After the raid, two Iraqi MiG-23MSs intercepted a pair of IRIAF fighters and apparently shot one of them down near the Iranian border. The wreckage of the F-4 was found the next day, together with detailed maps of the whole area that had been marked with Iraqi positions. The IrAF was stunned by the precision of Iranian intelligence, which seemed to be based not only on photo-reconnaissance sorties carried out before the war, but also on the latest operations. Even when their intelligence was not particularly current, the Iranians maintained a good picture of enemy positions.

Raids deep inside Iraq, which usually encountered little more than wild anti-aircraft fire, caught the attention of international observers. Yet operations crucial to the outcome of ground battles along the long frontline often passed unnoticed. This was mainly due to the fact that the Iranians were reluctant to present a clear picture of their operations to the outside world, but also because the fighting was so fierce that no reporters dared approach the front.

By 30 September the Iranians had halted the Iraqi invasion at Dezful, Ahwaz and Abadan. Both the army and the air force had paid a heavy price for this success, with many aircraft and helicopters being downed or damaged and their crews killed or wounded. However, the losses did not approach even half the 100 aircraft claimed by the Iraqis.

ENTER THE F-4D

Although increasingly occupied with BAI strikes and close air support missions for the ground troops, the IRIAF nevertheless had to continue striking deep into Iraq in order to keep its oil exporting industry, and therefore its ability to fund the war, under constant pressure. On 4 October, the deepest penetration strike into Iraq so far was flown by two F-4Ds armed with Paveway I laser-guided bombs. Thanks to careful planning and disciplined low-level flying, the two Phantom IIs penetrated 150 miles into Iraq without being detected by IrAF air defences.

The crews attacked the Buzargan oil pumping station 32 miles north of Nasseriyah with GBU-10 LGBs. Launched from a range of five miles, both bombs scored direct hits, destroying an estimated 20,000 metric tons of Iraqi crude oil. Maj Daryush 'Z' recalls;

'The Shah had been greatly impressed by the USAF's use of laser-guided bombs in Vietnam, and as soon as Iran got the go-ahead to order the F-4D, talks were also started on equipping our Phantom IIs with them. The IIAF wanted to buy the newest American laser package, known as the "Pave Knife", which was the most sophisticated laser designation system in the world at the time. The Pave Knife system was not actually built into the Phantom II, instead being carried in a large pod mounted on the left inner wing pylon. F-4s equipped with it had a TV screen in the rear cockpit, which transmitted a picture directly from a movable television camera

mounted in the pod, making Pave Knife very accurate. Pave Knife-equipped Phantom IIs could designate targets for their own bombs, as well as those dropped by other F-4s. However, the Pentagon would not allow this system to be sold to Iran. What the Americans did agree to sell us was a limited number of the older, less sophisticated, but still top secret, laser systems that Pave Knife was replacing in USAF service, namely the AVQ-9 Pave Light/Paveway I.

'The Paveway I laser designator box had been nicknamed the "Zot Box" by US pilots, and this name followed it into Iranian service. The Zot system featured great accuracy and reliability, and we were very proud to be the first air force trusted by the Americans with this equipment.

The Zot system was a semi-active 'man in the loop' laser unit that relied on the F-4D backseater to visually acquire targets through a high-powered telescope mounted on the canopy rail. The field of view was limited, but once the backseater had the target lined up in the telescope's cross hairs, he would turn on the laser pod and follow the target with the telescope, while shooting a pulsating laser beam at it, thus designating it for the seeker heads mounted on the bombs. Another F-4D trailing close behind the Zot-equipped Phantom II then released the bomb, or bombs, within a prescribed area surrounding the beam known as the "laser basket." This enabled the bomb's optical seeker to see and home in on the spot of laser light where the designator beam shone on the target.

'The Paveway I system worked very well, although it did have its share of problems. It took at least two F-4s to fly LGB missions, and the loss of either of these aircraft would effectively end the mission. The other problem was that the Zot-equipped F-4D had to hold a stable flight path at medium or high altitude as it marked the target for the LGB-dropping Phantom II, and

A classic two-ship formation of Iranian F-4Ds at low level. Although written-off by most western observers, who suspected that these older Phantom II were being used as a spares source for the F-4Es, the F-4Ds soldiered on with the 71st TFW. Indeed, this unit achieved considerable success with the aircraft throughout the war (*authors' collection*)

In the early 1970s, the AVQ-9 'Zot Box' was a top-secret piece of equipment. Its delivery to the IIAF was considered highly sensitive, and no photographs were ever taken of it in Iranian service. This shot of the mounting on the rear canopy rail of an F-4D belonging to the USAF's 8th TFW during the Vietnam War is therefore the only way of illustrating the 'Zot' (*US DoD*)

then stay in close proximity to the target while it was holding its marker on it. The laser had to remain "locked on" until the LGBs had impacted the target. This meant that if you were not suppressing Iraqi air defences, the Zot F-4D became an easy target for the enemy.

'We had plenty of LGBs on hand at the start of the war with Iraq, but we were never able to use them properly. This was primarily because our F-4D units had only 15 backseaters trained in the deployment of the Paveway I, and only about half of these again had ever guided a live bomb. Furthermore, we could not effectively suppress Iraqi air defences long enough to allow our F-4Ds to safely hold laser lock-on on a target and in turn aim and then drop an LGB with any degree of accuracy. As a result of these problems, a disproportionate number of F-4Ds were being lost when sent on LGB missions.'

Virtually all surviving F-4Ds were heavily involved in retaliatory missions following the surprise Iraqi invasion in September 1980. The 306th TFS, commanded by Capt Reza Mohamad, had between two and four F-4Ds deployed at Vahdati air base, and these aircraft were assigned high priority targets such as bunkers, bridges and power plants due to their LGB capability, as Daryush 'Z' explains;

'Flying in pairs, one F-4D would mark the target with the laser designator – AVQ-9 Pave Light – while the other F-4D would launch the LGB. The IRIAF had 300 GBU-10A kits at the start of the war, and these were used to turn the Mk 84 iron bomb into an LGB. During training, we had scored hits with eight out of ten LGBs, although these peacetime flights were not opposed by AAA, MiG-21s and SA-6s! We soon found out that no matter how plucky our pilots were, bravery was no shield against these Iraqi weapons. Less than 30 days after the start of the war, five F-4Ds had been lost and three other damaged during missions in which LGBs were used. Little damage had in turn been inflicted on Iraqi targets. By comparison, during the same time only one F-4D was lost and two others damaged on iron bomb missions. As a result of these losses, all LGB missions were stopped, unless ordered by IRIAF high command. The hard truth was that at the rate aircraft were being lost on LGB missions, in less than 60 days there would be no F-4Ds left in the IRIAF.'

RF-4E MISSIONS

On 12 October the 1st TFW at Mehrabad was ordered to photograph the headquarters of the Iraqi Ba'th Party, the Presidential Palace, the National Parliament and several key bridges in Baghdad. To fly this extremely dangerous mission, Maj Bahram Ikani, an experienced RF-4E pilot with many missions inside Iraq to his credit, was chosen. Crossing the border at very low altitude, he followed a carefully-selected route to avoid Iraqi military positions. He was not detected before he reached Baghdad, and there was no opposition. However, in order to take his photos Ikani had to pull up to 1300 ft, at which height all hell broke loose.

The RF-4E needed 1 minute 40 seconds to cover all the targets in and around Baghdad whilst flying at 625 mph, during which time all available Iraqi anti-aircraft guns and missiles (ranging from ZPU-14-2s to ZSU-57-2s and from SA-2s to SA-6s) were firing at him. Evading everything, the Phantom II thundered away from Baghdad, but then its radar detected two Iraqi MiG-23 fighters closing from ahead. Ikani had no choice but to increase speed and flash past the MiGs, which turned in behind him and began to chase the RF-4. The Iranian pilot responded with a hard banking turn of his own, losing height down to just 30 ft.

Seconds later Ikani came under SAM attack, an SA-3 flying past his aircraft and hitting the ground just behind him. The Phantom II trembled and violently veered to the left when hit by the shockwave from the exploding missile, the buffeting rupturing one of its fuel tanks. Ikani rolled out of his turn and continued at high speed toward the border.

The two MiG-23s were soon within gun range, and they duly opened fire. Although Ikani could not fly any lower, the Iraqis in turn could not fire their missiles, as they would hit the ground as soon as they left the rails. He continued to speed

away, manoeuvring only when faced by obstacles on the ground. When just 20 miles from the border, Ikani realised his chances of getting home were now very slim, as fuel was streaming from the ruptured tank, and the rate of consumption at the speed needed to keep both MiG-23s behind him was very high.

The dispersal revetments at al-Taqqadum air base, near Lake Habbaniyah. are clearly visible in this low-altitude RF-4E photograph, probably taken by Maj Bahram Ikani during his epic 12 October 1980 mission. Two MiG-23MSs could not be scrambled or hidden in time, and they can be seen in the revetments. The entrances to the extensive underground facilities are also visible in the background (*authors' collection*)

A dramatic reconnaissance photograph of an Iraqi logistics centre, taken by the RF-4E of Maj Bahram Ikani. Note the Phantom II's shadow in the bottom right corner. The jet's left wing has been damaged by ground fire, leaving fuel and smoke streaming in the Phantom II's wake. Despite this, Ikani and his WSO remained with the aircraft and flew it safely back to Iran (*authors' collection*)

Destination Iraq – a Boeing 707-3J9C tanker supplies four Phantom IIs with fuel prior to the fighter-bombers pushing into Iraqi airspace on yet another strike mission. This photograph was taken by the pilot of the leading Phantom II from a trailing flight, which was awaiting its turn to top off its tanks (*authors' collection*)

Ikani was determined to save his precious cargo, however, and luck then turned in his favour. The MiGs broke off their attack after reaching their 'bingo' fuel point, and moments later Ikani declared an emergency and gained altitude to save fuel. Realising that the RF-4 was in serious trouble, the pilot of a waiting Boeing 707 tanker flew into Iraqi airspace despite the presence of enemy fighters.

While still 18 miles from the Boeing, Ikani's fuel gauges showed just 600 lbs of fuel remaining, and it was clear that the engines could flame out at any moment. Approaching the tanker, he plugged into the refuelling boom on his first try. Turning slowly round during the refuelling process, both jets continued in formation for home. After landing, Ikani counted 17 shrapnel holes in his RF-4, one of which was just four inches from the refuelling probe. Despite his outstanding wartime service with the IRIAF, Maj Bahram Ikani was executed by the Islamic regime soon after the conflict ended.

Four days after Ikani returned from his reconnaissance mission, two F-4Ds, toting M-117 bombs and ALQ-87(V)-3 ECM pods, and escorted by two F-14 Tomcats and a Boeing 707 tanker, took off to attack Iraqi Habbaniyah (Tammouz) air base, some 70 miles west of Baghdad.

Maj Daryush 'Z' describes the background to these operations;

The KRB3MR bridge spanning the Karun River was bombed by two 306th TFS F-4Ds in mid-October using the 'Zot'/GBU-10 Paveway I LGB combination, halting an Iraqi advance which had threatened to drive deeply into Khuzestan Province. The Iraqis later crossed the Karun, but they had to mount a large operation to do so, exposing troops and vehicles to further sustained IRIAF attacks. Here, two Iraqi soldiers inspect the damage to the bridge after it was hit by the GBU-10s (*authors' collection*)

'The IRIAF command infrastructure after 1979 was only a shadow of its former self, and our intelligence services were almost non-existent at the start of the war with Iraq. Therefore, it took our air force some weeks to get any real "co-ordination and momentum" in order to increase both mission rates and the number of strikes against important targets. With the increase in intelligence came an improvement in the mission briefings. Typically, they would be extraordinarily detailed and well-planned, although I also experienced a ten-minute briefing in which very little information was passed to individual aircrews. On occasion, we had much to study before the actual mission, for we could not just jump into a fighter and bomb Iraq without extremely good planning. We had to study maps, plot the best course to evade known Iraqi defences and compute all this so as to reach the target, bomb it and still have enough fuel to return to Iran. We also had to familiarise ourselves with call signs, radio frequencies and weapon loads for the mission, and then learn the best altitudes and airspeeds to fly during that mission.

'We had few uniform goals for mission planning at the start of the war – pin down the Iraqi army, defend Iran from the Iraqi air force and attack their airfields, refineries, fuel depots, ammunition dumps, arms factories and chemical storage facilities.

'Most of these targets were located in the area between Baghdad, Mousel, Kirkuk and Tikrit. Needless to say, this area was defended by the best aircraft and weapons that the Iraqis had. We also attacked several Iraqi air bases so as to put pressure on the IrAF to defend them, rather than attack Iran. Although we knew that attacking an airfield was bar far the most dangerous mission that we could fly, to complete such a sortie always did wonders for our morale – the Iraqis were inferior to us in terms of equipment and training, but their base facilities were excellent.'

Returning to the 16 October mission on Habbaniyah, after refuelling at 13,000 ft over the front, both F-4Ds lost height and crossed the Iraqi border along the route taken by RF-4 pilot Maj Ikani four days earlier. Due to the potent air defences that ringed Baghdad, it was decided that both jets should fly directly over the Iraqi capital. Reaching the city without interference, the crews then encountered serious opposition in the form of SAMs and IrAF fighters. The first F-4D was immediately shot down, either by an SA-6 or by MiG-23s, and the crew captured – it was one of the first

D-models to be lost in the campaign. The second jet evaded one missile by making an eye-watering 11g turn, but as it was clear that an attack on Habbaniyah was now impossible, the crew then headed for their secondary target – the Al-Bakr oil refinery.

This attack saw a string of M-117 bombs hit the target, and as the lone Phantom II set course towards the Iranian border, it was again intercepted by two MiG-23MSs. The Iraqis fired several R-13 missiles at the F-4D, and the Iranian pilot

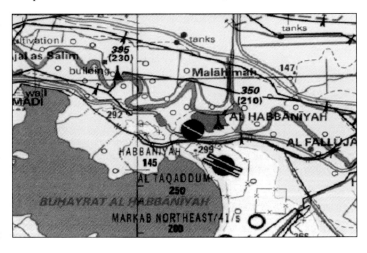

This map shows the position of the IrAF Tammouz (formerly RAF Habbaniyah) and al-Taqqadum air bases, some 40 miles west of Baghdad, which were targeted by two F-4Ds on 16 October 1980 in one of the longest strikes flown during the entire war (*NIMA Tactical Pilotage Chart 1:500,000 scale*)

An Iraqi SA-6 site near Baghdad. This Soviet-built missile system proved deadly in Iraqi service – just as it had done when used by the Israelis in 1973 – especially against the less sophisticated Iranian Northrop F-5E/F Tiger IIs, which lacked the Phantom IIs' comprehensive ECM suites. Even the latter provided no guarantee of safety from SAMs, for the Iraqis did manage to surprise Iranian F-4 crews from time to time, and in such cases the first warning of SA-6 activity usually came when a jet was blown out of the sky. This happened to two F-4Ds during a raid on Tammouz air base on 12 October 1980 (*authors' collection*)

responded by dropping his external tanks and accelerating to maximum speed 'on the deck'. Shortly afterwards, the MiGs broke off their pursuit due to a shortage of fuel. The F-4D was also now low on fuel, and the crew declared an emergency and prepared to eject over enemy territory. Unwilling to leave their comrades to their fate, the supporting tanker and escorting F-14s flew into Iraq to provide assistance. When the retreating fighter made contact with the tanker it had just 350 lbs of fuel left.

This operation had probably been the longest-ranging mission performed by the IRIAF up to that date. Indeed, the distance involved was only to be exceeded by two later strikes against the H-2 oil pumping station, halfway between al-Ruthbah and Baghdad, and the H-3 air base complex in western Iraq. According to Maj Daryush 'Z', there was a simple reason why F-4 crews were able to reach targets so deep inside Iraq without being detected. 'We had about 60 routes into Iraq that allowed us to enter and leave enemy territory without being detected by radar.'

'SILKWORM' STRIKE, BIRD STRIKE

During October, the F-4s from TFB 6 continued their 'mini-war' against Iraqi installations in the Basrah area which were disrupting Iranian shipping in the northern Persian Gulf. One such mission saw crews briefed to attack three HY-2G 'Silkworm' ('Seersucker') missile sites behind Shoaibah, which the Iraqis had been using to attack Iranian vessels travelling to and from Bandar Khomeini. The mission was to be flown by a solitary F-4E, crewed by newly-promoted Maj Yassini and Capt Eqdam. Basrah's electrical generating facility east of the city was designated as the secondary target in case the primary one could not be hit.

Setting a north-westerly course, Yassini climbed to cruise altitude to conserve fuel, but before reaching the border he descended to 325 ft, increasing speed during the dive towards the palm groves that surrounded Abadan. Passing the Shatt al-Arab, Yassini further decreased his altitude before thundering over the Faw Peninsula and the Um Qassr marshes. This circuitous route helped avoid early detection by Iraqi radar.

Eqdam, meanwhile, was busy in the rear cockpit checking his instruments and threat warning devices. Suddenly, a SAM was detected coming straight for the Phantom II, but Yassini made a well-timed evasive manoeuvre and the missile flashed harmlessly by. A few moments later everything went dark. After about 20 seconds Eqdam regained consciousness. The aircraft was climbing in a 50-degree bank to starboard.

When flying at such low altitudes, pilots instinctively kept the aircraft trimmed slightly nose-high so that if anything happened they could immediately climb and avoid hitting the ground. Eqdam called Yassini on the intercom but he received no reply, even though he knocked his pilot's shoulder with the checklist clipboard. It was only then that he noticed flesh and bird feathers all round the front cockpit – they had hit a flock of seagulls and the jet was badly damaged.

As the pilot was either unconscious or dead, Eqdam took over using the F-4E's basic rear cockpit controls. He immediately called the GCI. 'Ababil to radar! Do you read me?' An unknown voice replied. 'Ababil, this is Oqaab (Eagle). Stand by.' Somebody else was responding. The call from the rear cockpit of the crippled Phantom II had been heard by the crew of an F-14 patrolling nearby. 'Are you in trouble?' Eqdam replied, 'Our aeroplane is damaged. Apparently, the pilot has lost consciousness or has been killed'. He was told, 'Stay calm. Try to regain control of the aeroplane. I'm coming to you'.

Eqdam's call had been received in the Tomcat flown by Capt Mohamad-Hashem Ale-Agha, himself an experienced F-4 pilot. Minutes later he closed on the damaged Phantom II and positioned himself on its wing. Ale-Agha called, 'Ababil, continue this course. Be careful not to eject. Your parachute has been opened and is spread above the fuselage. Your aeroplane looks like an AWACS'. Eqdam replied, 'Thanks. I'll try to control the aircraft, but I don't know what has happened to Yassini'. Ale-Agha replied, 'Stay calm and continue on this course. I'm right behind you, don't worry'.

But Eqdam had plenty to worry about. Despite the throttles being set at 100 per cent power, the engines were pushing the Phantom II at only 180 knots – barely enough to prevent the jet from stalling. The intercom was out and the cockpit was a mess, but shortly after crossing back into Iran Eqdam noticed movement in the front cockpit – Yassini was alive. The force of the collision and the flying glass had ripped away his helmet and visor. Yassini was covered with blood, but otherwise seemed okay.

Not being able to eject, Eqdam flew slowly back to Bushehr. Once in the circuit, Yassini was able to take over and they landed safely. The crew were carefully helped out of the shattered cockpit, which looked as if someone had taken an axe to it. The windscreen and canopy were shattered, there were dents all over the fuselage and 150 blades and stators in the right engine had been destroyed. A later inspection revealed that both J79 engines had been so badly damaged that they had to be written off. To the casual bystander it seemed impossible that an aircraft which had been so badly damaged could fly over 125 miles back to its base and land safely. The F-4 was eventually repaired and returned to service.

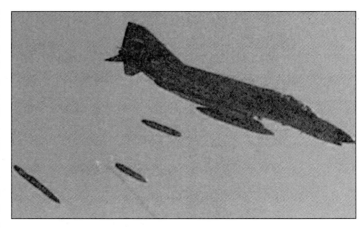

The IRIAF had a huge stock of napalm-filled bombs, and they were used extensively throughout the war. This F-4E is seen dropping four BLU-27s early in the conflict (*authors' collection*)

NOT A PERFECT MISSION

During October the Phantom IIs flew hundreds of combat sorties as the IRIAF struggled to halt the Iraqi invasion, and eventually the enemy advance was halted, but at a heavy cost in men and machinery. One of the final missions of that month saw two F-4D crews from the 71st TFW tasked with flying a close air support mission for troops engaging armour near Ahwaz, in the Jofeir – an area known to be heavily defended by AAA.

For this mission the aircraft staged through Nojeh, taking off at 1420 hrs. The pilots had been carefully briefed about their target, the crews being told that the Iraqi units were well camouflaged and protected by a heavy concentration of anti-aircraft guns. With Iranian forces very close by, the bombs had to be dropped with precision so as to avoid friendly casualties. Approaching Ahwaz, the element leader noticed several targets, so he made a sharp, high-g climbing right turn in order to rapidly gain altitude. His wingman followed behind him. Pushing over and diving on the target, the leader talked his wingman down by relaying information on the nearby topography so as to aid his aim.

While this was going on, Iraqi 23 mm and 57 mm AAA grew in intensity, with puffs of smoke appearing all around the F-4s – the close explosions of the heavier 57 mm shells suggested that they were radar-guided.

The leader completed his bombing run and pulled safely out of his dive. Now it was his wingman's turn, the latter completing a 360-degree turn before climbing steeply in order to visually acquire the target – a group of tanks, surrounded by numerous anti-aircraft positions. He dived, rolled out and started his attack run. Tracers zipped all round the Phantom II, following its dive. Dust and smoke from the leader's bombs partially obscured the pilot's vision, but he was still able to select the SUU-23/A gun pod and work the Iraqi tanks over with 20 mm cannon fire. He then dropped his bombs directly on the target, after which he pulled into a tight right banking climb as planned. Less than five seconds into this manoeuvre the Phantom II suddenly lurched upwards and yawed out of control – it had obviously been hit somewhere beneath the tail and left wing. The left J79 engine caught fire and the aircraft was now leaving a trail of thick black smoke.

Still over enemy-held territory, the pilot elected to keep both engines in full afterburner in order to complete his hard right turn. The anti-aircraft fire was still heavy, the sky being filled with clouds of black smoke. Leaving the target area behind, the pilot turned off the left afterburner and throttled the right engine back to 85 per cent power. But now there was a fresh problem – a loss of hydraulic pressure caused by fluid seeping from damaged control lines. This caused the jet to veer to the left, requiring great effort to hold it on course. The leader flew alongside his wingman and made a quick assessment of the damage – the tail, left wing, right main gear door and the whole under-fuselage were damaged. There was also a major fuel leak, which could catch fire at any moment.

The leader recommended diversion to an emergency landing strip, but his wingman preferred to land at the nearest base – Vahdati – even if it lacked a barrier arrestor facility. The fuel leak worried both crews the most, for it meant that the aircraft could run dry at any moment. Short of fuel himself, the leader decided to leave the damaged Phantom II and fly straight back to base.

During his approach, the pilot of the damaged F-4 noticed that the landing gear would not fully extend, forcing him to employ emergency procedures which blew the gear down. Later, it was found that only the

right wheel had initially locked down properly, although the nose gear deployed after it was blown down. Once contact was made with the runway, the left main tyre burst and the heavily damaged right landing gear collapsed, causing the aircraft to veer slowly to the right. The pilot tried to use engine thrust to keep the jet under control and maintain a straight path, but the jet eventually ran away. Still using the engines to control the aircraft, the pilot then attempted a left turn, but after using all 10,000 ft of the runway, the F-4 overshot at slow speed, ground-looping before coming to rest on the grass separating the two runways.

By then the Phantom II's tyre-shorn wheels had caught fire, although the base fire-crew arrived swiftly and soon extinguished the blaze. A subsequent inspection showed extensive damage to the right and left main landing gear. Stripped of its engines and other heavy parts, the damaged F-4D was duly slung beneath a CH-47C and transported back to its home base, where it was returned to service after months of repair work.

F-4D 3-6711 was badly damaged during an attack on Iraqi troops near Ahwaz in mid-October 1980. The aircraft was hit in the left wing and engine, starting a fire, although the pilot managed to limp back to Vahdati (TFB 4), where the left oleo collapsed on landing and the right tyre burst. Note the empty TER under the starboard wing and the SUU-23A gun pod, knocked out of its fastenings, under the centreline. Surprisingly, the nose gear remained intact, with neither tyre bursting, despite some very hard braking and several high-speed turning manoeuvres on the runway (*authors' collection*)

THE SHAH'S PILOTS

By late November relentless pounding by the Iranians had not only stopped the Iraqis from driving deeper into the country, but also sapped the invaders' offensive capability. With scores of vehicles and many supply depots bombed and rocketed into obliteration, the IRIAF had bought time for Iranian ground forces to organise their defences. A coherent frontline was finally established, and the Iraqi drive into Khuzestan and other parts of Iran halted. Maj Daryush 'Z' recalls;

'No one knows the sacrifices and efforts of the IRIAF and IRIAA (Islamic Republic of Iran Army Aviation) during the first months of the war. I can say with pride that during the first year we stopped the Iraqis at the Karun River. The provincial capital of Ahwaz was saved from Iraqi capture by the Iranian Army and revolutionary guards, with strong air support by the IRIAF and IRIAA, which pinned down the Iraqi tanks and artillery just seven miles from the city. Such a move prevented them from massing for new attacks. The IRIAF and IRIAA also stopped the Iraqi bid to vanquish the city of Dezful and the key air base at Vahdati (TFB 4), which in turn stopped the Iraqis from launching a pincer assault on Ahwaz. The IRIAF also bombed every new Iraqi Army unit that drove through the captured Iranian border town of Qassr-e Shirin into Iran. Iraqi troops would immediately realise that they were not welcome in Iran, and that we were watching them. We did all this with the "Shah's bad blood" still running in our veins.'

Although additional groups of pilots had been released from prisons to reinforce IRIAF ranks following the Iraqi invasion, their position remained precarious because their long term future was by no means secure. Daryush 'Z' continues;

'Westerners never truly understood – or had a hard time understanding – the feelings of the new Iranian regime towards what it called the "Shah's army and air force". Time and again, the government publicly stated that the "blood of the Shah was in the army and air force", and it made every effort to rid itself of this bad "Shah blood". To outside observers, such "kill or imprison" statements frequently led to the misunderstanding that the IRIAF – including its Phantom II-equipped units – was left without leaders and personnel, and was therefore unable to fight the war. In fact, the new Iranian leaders knew and understood very well that these previously unwanted military personnel were badly needed to defend both them and Iran against the invasion. To this day, many of us still find it hard to believe that the invading Iraqi army saved our lives from our own government.'

Upon their release from prison, several IRIAF officers complained about the treatment they had received. Indeed, legendary F-4 pilot Capt Dowran soon run into trouble both with the IRIAF High Command and the government after he spoke out about the severe torture and murder of so many of the best ex-IIAF pilots and senior

For much of October 1980, IRIAF F-4 units attacked Iraqi troops along the frontline, inflicting extensive losses on the enemy. The Phantom II crews also worked very closely with Islamic Republic of Iran Army Aviation (IRIAA), which flew Bell 214C Isfahan transport helicopters (built to Iranian requirements) and Bell AH-1J Cobra Internationals. Both forces suffered heavy losses during this campaign whilst stopping the invasion and neutralising the Iraqi Army's offensive power (*Bell Textron, via authors*)

officers, several of whom had left the air force before being arrested. Dowran realised that the way the regime and the clergy were handling the situation could cost Iran the war, so he wrote a letter of protest to the Iranian government, which not only explained the situation currently facing the air force, but also the reasons why the IRIAF – and its Phantoms II – had actually survived to date. He wrote;

'The arrest and murder of our military pilots and command officers by religious decree must come to an end as soon as possible. The participation in this war by our air force without these pilots and leaders is suicidal, and may very well already have cost Iran this war. Forced confessions from our pilots will not fill our cockpits and force the Iraqis from the borders of our beloved nation. These pilots you allow to be arrested and so callously executed are not insurgents or rebels against you, but loyal Iranian military pilots by nature. Each pilot and command officer you allow to be executed is a major victory for our sworn enemy: Iraq.'

It is not clear if this letter influenced the situation, but in October another group of imprisoned pilots was released. Losses suffered during the first month of the war, combined with a lack of experienced commanders, had forced the regime in Tehran to free them. Together with the Iraqis, President Bani-Sadr had become the savour of many imprisoned pilots who were now able help to defend Iran. The feelings of many newly-freed pilots could be summed by one who declared, 'I was released from prison and ordered to fight Iraqis, who had actually saved me from certain death'. Another former Phantom II pilot stated;

'I was in jail from February 1980 until October 1980, when by the order of the Commander-in-Chief of the Armed Forces, President Bani-Sadr, I was released from prison and ordered to be rehabilitated. The "new" IRIAF needed IIAF pilots in order to survive. Rehabilitation for me would consist mainly of a number of long lectures by loyal IRIAF officers and religious leaders. They talked about the "evils of the Shah and his loyal followers". Upon my complete rehabilitation, which took about five days, I was allowed to see my family for three days. Then I was sent to TFB 4 to fly F-5E/Fs – and later F-4Es – for the air force.'

Bani-Sadr was later blamed for pardoning too many pilots, as a few of them defected, along with their aircraft, at the first chance they got.

Another of the 'Shah's Pilots', or just an Iranian patriot? Capt Farassyabi is seen shortly after qualifying to fly the F-4E in the late 1970s (authors' collection)

Flying an F-4E of the 61st TFW, Capt Mahmoud Shadmanbakht was shot down and killed, together with his WSO, 1Lt Abolfazl Mahdiyar, during an attack on the port of Faw on 24 October 1980. Shadmanbakht is seen here with F-4E 3-6591 just prior to the outbreak of war (*authors' collection*)

WHEN EAGLES FALL

The fighting along the front had calmed down by late November 1980, as the Iranians made preparations for the first major counter-offensives of the war. The IRIAF, meanwhile, maintained the pressure on Iraqi infrastructure with further bombing raids. One of the most spectacular attacks was Operation *Morvarid*, which targeted two offshore oil rigs in the northern Persian Gulf. The al-Omayeh and al-Bakr platforms were attacked in a series of devastating raids by helicopter-borne commandos and Iranian naval vessels, supported by Phantom IIs from TFB 6. During these attacks, the F-4s not only downed three MiG-23s, but also sank more than a dozen Iraqi missile and torpedo-boats using AGM-65 Mavericks. One aircraft, flown by 1Lt Hassan Moftakhari and 2Lt Mohamad-Kazem Roosta, was lost on 29 November.

The IRIAF spent most of December preparing for the New Year offensive, although this did not stop it from launching fresh strikes against IrAF bases. One such mission, flown from Nojeh on 29 December, saw Capt Mohamad-Yousef Ahmad-beigi chosen to lead the second pair in a section of four F-4E which were to strike the football stadium at Badreh, which was being used by the Iraqi Army Air Corps (IrAAC) as a base for several of its helicopters. Ahmadbeigi had been trained by the USAF to fly the F-4, and had served at Bandar Abbas prior to being transferred to Shahrokhi/ Nojeh in response to the uprising in Kur-destan earlier in the year. By December he had flown many successful missions over Iraq.

The IRIAF used at least two types of US-built cluster bomb units, both of which were supplied by Israel. This photograph shows the unexploded bomblets contained within one such weapon, dropped by Iranian F-4s during an attack on Iraqi positions in the central frontline (*authors' collection*)

Together with the BL 755, the Mk 82 bomb fitted with Snakeye retarding fins was the Iranian F-4 pilots' preferred air-to-ground weapon, mainly because it could be deployed with great precision during high-speed, low altitude passes, as demonstrated by this photograph, taken during a training mission by F-4Es from Mehrabad (TFB 1). The Mk 82 was used against all kinds of targets (*authors' collection*)

This latest strike was to depart at noon, with Capt Iraj Ossareh, who had just arrived from Bandar Abbas, as mission leader. Ahmadbeigi's wingman was to be Capt Asqar Rezvani, and all four aircraft participating in the strike were to be armed with BL 755 CBUs and Mk 82 Snakeyes. During planning for the mission there had been numerous disagreements between Ossareh and Ahmadbeigi. These arose due to Ossareh's unfamiliarity with the terrain, the mission leader insisting that the second pair of F-4s arrive over the target 15 minutes after the attack by the first jets so as to avoid

A view of Qayyarah air base, near Mousel, in the autumn of 1980, courtesy of an IRIAF RF-4Es. An IrAF MiG-21 can be seen near the hardened shelter in the lower left corner. During the war the IRIAF attacked any Iraqi airfield at which concentrations of aircraft or helicopters could be identified. Such bases were heavily defended, and represented highly dangerous targets (*authors' collection*)

any possible mid-air collisions. Ahmadbeigi was concerned that Iraqi air defences would be well and truly alerted by then, leaving the second element as sitting ducks. With this in mind, he urged that just a pair of F-4s be despatched so as to achieve more flexibility over the target. Ossareh, however, insisted that the mission had to be flown by four Phantom IIs.

Maintaining radio silence, the flight took off on time and headed for the target in a low altitude tactical formation. Leaving the Iranian mountains and canyons behind them, they crossed the border. Ossareh deviated off course and Ahmadbeigi broke radio silence to warn him. The flight then descended to 70 ft. About 15 miles into Iraq, the formation reached its first waypoint. Preparing to turn, Ahmadbeigi saw a group of military vehicles and road construction machinery in front of him. He decided to drop a bomb on them so that he could activate his gun camera and gather some intelligence on their activities.

Ahmadbeigi dropped what he thought was just one Snakeye, and was rewarded with a huge fireball, but his backseater, Capt Ayoub Hussein-nejadi, then reported that the jet's entire bombload had been released! This was confirmed by Ahmadbeigi's weapon status indicator. At first he decided to continue to the objective and strafe the helicopters with his gun, but he then changed his mind when he realised that he needed to conserve his ammunition for any possible aerial combat.

Just as Ahmadbeigi began to radio his wingman to tell him of his decision, he felt AAA striking the belly of his aircraft. Flying at 540-560 knots, the Phantom II jolted violently, and moments later it was hit in the left rear by a SAM. The aircraft started pitching up and down, and as the pilot struggled to retain control, a second missile slammed into the right rear of the jet, causing the F-4 to pitch up even more sharply. Ahmadbeigi was unable to level off, and the g-forces caused him to black out. He regained consciousness just as the aircraft was diving steeply at an angle of 70-80 degrees towards the ground. The cockpit then decompressed, making a noise like water being poured on a fire. Ahmadbeigi then tried to pull the aircraft out of its dive, but the controls would not respond.

By the time he finally ejected, the pilot could clearly see bushes on the ground. He felt hot and weightless, and was then pushed into the seat.

Ahmadbeigi's parachute opened, and bullets began whizzing past him as he floated down. He hit the ground hard, badly injuring his arm. Ahmadbeigi was immediately captured by two Iraqi officers armed with Kalashnikovs, and in English, they ordered him to get up. Turning his head, Ahmadbeigi could see the wreckage of his burning Phantom II. Several hundred yards away he saw another piece of the aircraft, with Husseinnejadi's parachute lying nearby. At first Ahmadbeigi feared that his backseater had been killed, but then he saw him being beaten by Iraqi soldiers. As the pilot pleaded for his comrade, the officers pulled the WSO away from the soldiers, and both men were taken to the regional headquarters. They were separated, and an Iraqi major began questioning Ahmadbeigi;

'Are you Iranian?'

'Yes.'

'Why did you crash?'

'My aircraft had a technical problem.'

'Technical problem? Or were you shot down?'

'It doesn't matter. I'm in your hands now.'

'How many aircraft were you?'

'Four.'

'Where were you intending to attack?'

'Badreh football field.'

'You mean people?'

'No!'

'So why a football field?'

'Because your helicopters had been parked there (he could not conceal the identity of his target because he had been unable to destroy his kneeboard, to which the route and mission maps were attached).

'How do you know?'

'I don't know how, I just carry out my orders.'

After ten years of imprisonment and torture in Iraq, Lt Gen Mohamad-Yousef Ahmadbeigi was released in 1990 and returned to the IRIAF to fly Phantom IIs once again (*authors' collection*)

'How many aircraft were you?'

'I told you, four.'

'Do you know that we shot down all four?'

'No. You just shot my aircraft down. The others escaped.

'How do you know?'

'Because I talked to them and told them I was going to bale out (he was actually bluffing, since he had not had time to do so).

'Where did you have breakfast?'

'I guess I'll have lunch in Baghdad.'

'Ha… Ha… You're a smart captain. Where were you trained?'

'United States.'

'United States? The Great Satan?'

'Yeah. United States, the Great Satan.'

Both prisoners were then taken by car to the Ministry of Defence in Baghdad, where they were kept together with some other Iranian PoWs in separate cells. Two days later, Ahmadbeigi was taken to al-Rashid air base in southern Baghdad for interrogation, apparently by an intelligence major (or wing commander) and two IrAF pilot captains. The interrogation followed the by now familiar pattern;

'Name?'

'Ahmadbeigi, Mohamad-Yousef.'

'How many aircraft were you?'

'Four aircraft.'

'Do you know that we've shot down all four?'

'No. Only I was hit.'

'How do you know?'

'I informed them while ejecting.'

'No. We've shot all four down. What were you going to attack?'

'You should know it by now if you've downed all four of us.'

'At what altitude did you enter Iraqi territory?'

'5000 ft.'

'5000 ft? Where were you trained?'

'United States.'

'How many flight hours?'

'About 1500 hours.'

'So you're a leader. Do you know Davoud Salman (Capt Davoud Salman was an F-4-pilot who had been shot down and captured several days earlier)?'

'Yes. Where is he? With you?'

'No, he's not. He's dead.'

'He's with you and he's okay.'

'How do you know he's okay?'

'I've heard his voice on Iraqi radio.'

'But he's dead.'

'No, he isn't.'

'We will kill you too.'

'It doesn't matter.'

At this point a general, who was apparently the base CO, came into the room and took over the questioning;

'Captain, I want correct answers. Write down for us the names of the fighter pilots of the 31st and 32nd Wings at Shahrokhi air base.

'Under the Geneva Convention, I need only tell you my name, rank, and place of service. You cannot expect me to give you any more.'

'If you don't write it for us, we'll cut your hand off.'

Shortly afterwards all but one of the Iraqi pilots left the room. He continued the interrogation on his own;

'Captain, I'm a pilot like you, but if you don't do what they ask they'll hurt you.'

'But you know we don't know anything. We just get orders to fly the missions and we do just that. Decisions come from above.'

'That's right. But tell me, how many aircraft are based at Shahrokhi?'

'I don't know, the number changes.'

'How does it change? Don't you know the number?'

'No, I don't know because there's a war and it changes every day.'

'At what speed did you enter Iraqi airspace?'

'300 knots.'

'At what altitude?'

'5000 ft.'

'5000 ft?

'Yes.'

'How many close friends have you?'

'We're all friends.'

'Do you know any base commanders?'

'No.'

'Why?'

'Because they're further down the road and we don't have much contact with them.

'What about Golchin (he was then the CO of Shahrokhi/Nojeh AB)?

'He's my commander. That's all.'

'Is he with the regime?'

'It isn't possible otherwise for a commander.'

'You write down the names of the Shahrokhi pilots or you'll be hurt.

'I'm not supposed to do that even if you cut off my hand.'

Then they brought in a list of Shahrokhi 32nd Wing pilots. Ahmadbeigi noticed that it originated from pre-revolution days, as it included the names of pilots executed after the failed Nojeh coup attempt.

'So if you already have the list, why are you asking me?'

'How do you know we have the 32nd Wing list?'

'Here it is.'

Like other PoWs, Ahmadbeigi was often tortured during his early days in captivity. But there were other hazards. Some PoWs were held at Rashid military police prison, which was once damaged by an Iranian surface-to-surface missile which landed just 500 yards from the prison wall.

The interrogation continued;

'When you're sent on a helicopter CAP, at what altitude are you held (this was a combat air patrol over the border to intercept enemy helicopters and provide cover for friendly helicopters and non-combat aircraft).'

'Helicopter CAP?'

'Yes.'

'It depends on the pilot.'

'How?'

'There are manuals for that – you pilots should know.'

'I want to know how you fly CAP for helicopters.'

'We just fly CAP – nothing in particular.'

'No captain! When YOU fly CAP, how do you do that, and at what speed and altitude?'

'I do it at 50 ft!'

'Captain! Then your first enemy will be the terrain. How can you fly helicopter CAP at 50 ft?'

'That's my technique. It's war and everybody should use his initiative to survive.'

Capt Ahmadbeigi spent ten years in captivity, and was listed by the IRIAF as missing in action. Released in 1990 and repatriated, he duly resumed flying F-4s. He now holds the rank of lieutenant general.

The crew of another Iranian Phantom II downed over Iraq enjoyed better luck than Mohamad-Yousef Ahmadbeigi. On the morning of 5 December several F-4s from TFB 3 launched an attack on Iraqi supply lines and communications installations south-east of the northern city of Suleimaniyah. During the course of the mission the F-4E flown by Maj Seyed-Jalil Pour-Rezai and 1Lt Bahman Soleimani was shot down by two missiles, forcing the crew to eject over the mountains near Darbandikhan – just 19 miles (30km) inside Iraq. After the downed crew's position was pinpointed by another F-4, a risky rescue operation was launched by a Bell 214A and two AH-1J Cobras, with fighters providing top cover.

Departing at 1400 hrs, the rescuers had only three hours of daylight in which to work. Cobra pilot Lt Ahmad Pishgah-Hadiyan was the search and rescue team leader. After taking off from Sar Pol-e Zahab, he led the team to the west, away from the crash site. Passing several mountains, the helicopters then flew back towards Darbandikhan over an open plain, circling the town to remain undetected. However, in cold and snowy weather, they almost overflew a concentration of 15 anti-aircraft guns and SAM emplacements.

Reaching the crash site, the helicopters pulled up and orbited the area to search for the downed crew. Hadiyan sighted a flare, but within minutes of setting course to retrieve the men two Iraqi vehicles were seen approaching. Both were destroyed by 20 mm gunfire from the second Cobra prior to the Bell 214 landing and retrieving the downed crewmen.

While talking to the pilot and WSO on tactical radio before the pick up, Hadiyan learned that the F-4 crew had failed to attack Iraqi reinforcements which were advancing towards the front. So the AH-1 pilot left the team and went after the Iraqi unit, returning well after sunset, having inflicted substantial casualties on the enemy troops.

THE TIDE TURNS

On the morning of 5 January 1981, Iran commenced Operation *Howeizeh* – its first major counteroffensive. Armoured units were deployed to smash through Iraqi lines and push westward across the Karkheh Plain towards Susangerd. However, difficult terrain, combined with a lack of co-ordination and intelligence, caused the operation to stop in the centre of the Iraqi deployment. In the days that followed, Phantom IIs from Bushehr and Nojeh repeatedly hit Iraqi armour, buying time for the re-organisation of Iranian ground units. In a series of fierce

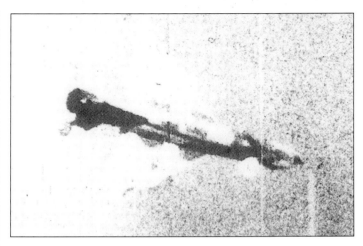

In April and May 1981, F-4Es from Nojeh and Vahdati claimed several kills against IrAF MiG-21MFs, including this one seen just moments prior to it being shot down by gunfire from very close range on 25 April 1981. Note the pipper held almost directly over the cockpit of the Iraqi fighter. Usually this would mean almost certain death for the pilot, but on this occasion 1Lt Dinmanruf managed to eject from the MiG (*authors' collection*)

air-to-ground battles, the F-4 crews destroyed scores of Iraqi tanks and SAM launchers primarily with AGM-65As and LGBs. But they also suffered losses to Iraqi SAMs (mainly SA-6s), which destroyed at least one F-4E and damaged an F-4D and several F-4Es.

In April, the Phantom IIs were involved in the next wave of strikes against Iraqi air power, with several of the enemy's leading airfields being hit. On the 4th, a formation of six F-4Es and two F-4Ds, supported by two Boeing 707 tankers, flew into Iraq to raid all three airfields within the H-3 complex. The strike was a total success. The Iraqis later claimed to have detected the formation coming from the direction of Syria en route to the target, although the Iranians achieved total surprise. The IRIAF destroyed a total of three An-12BP transports, a Tu-16 bomber, four MiG-21s, five Su-20/22s, eight MiG-23s, two Mirage F 1EQs and four helicopters.

On the 25th Ubeydah-Ibn-Jarrah air base was attacked by a formation of Phantom IIs from Vahdati (TFB 4). The target was badly hit, and during the following air battle a MiG-21 and a MiG-23 were shot down. Later, the Iraqis moved two squadrons of MiG-21MFs, equipped with French-made Matra R 550 Magic Mk 1 air-to-air missiles and flown by French-trained mercenary pilots, closer to the front. They immediately began to claim kills over the Vahdati Phantom IIs and F-5E Tiger IIs, and by mid-May, a dozen Iranian fighters had either been shot down or damaged, with heavy loss of life. On 15 May, the IRIAF deployed a squadron of F-14 Tomcats to Vahdati, and after they had shot down a MiG-21 during their first patrol over the area, the Iraqis were thrown back on the defensive, and did not reappear in this region for over a year.

After smaller operations by both sides during June and July 1981, the Iranians launched Operation *Samenol A'emeh* on 24 September. The objective was to raise the siege of Abadan. It was a huge success, causing severe Iraqi losses. Despite this, the regime in Baghdad remained determined not to withdraw its troops from Iran. Instead the IrAF was ordered to directly target the Iranian economy in an effort to destroy the country's ability to sustain the war. This campaign was to be maintained for the rest of the war, and it would have a decisive affect on the outcome of the conflict, as well the future development of the IrAF.

In the weeks leading up to the commencement of the strategic bombing offensive, the Iranians inflicted further heavy losses on the Iraqis in a series of air battles and airfield strikes in November and December 1981. More than 20 MiGs and Sukhois were destroyed.

Amassing further forces in March 1982, the Iranians began their largest operation to date – *Fat'holmobin*. F-4s from Nojeh and Bushehr temporary deployed to Vahdati to fly intensive airfield strikes and interdiction missions, again causing heavy losses to the Iraqis. In one attack, a complete Iraqi armoured division was decimated by (*text continues on page 62*)

COLOUR PLATES

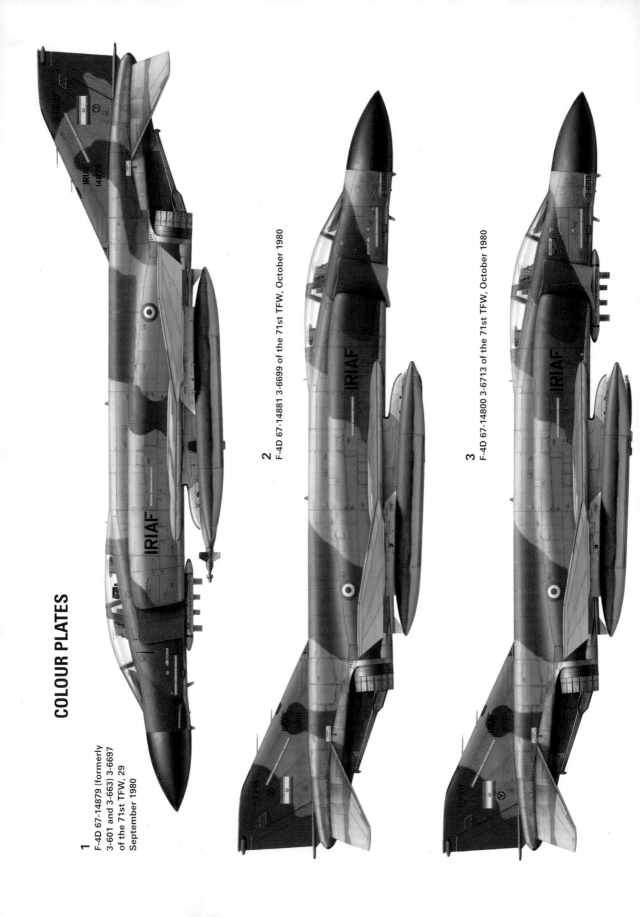

1
F-4D 67-14879 (formerly
3-601 and 3-663) 3-6697
of the 71st TFW, 29
September 1980

2
F-4D 67-14881 3-6699 of the 71st TFW, October 1980

3
F-4D 67-14800 3-6713 of the 71st TFW, October 1980

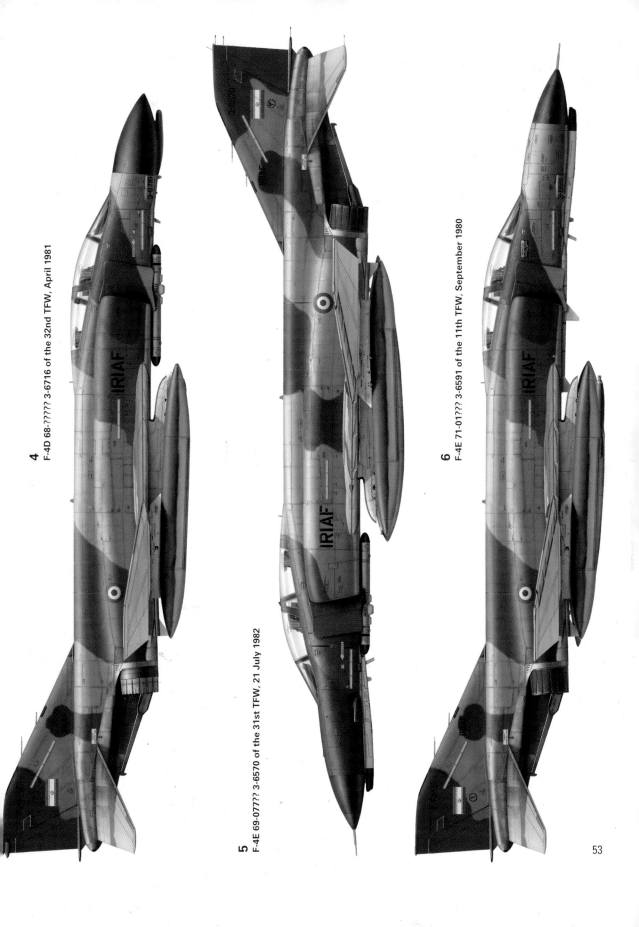

4
F-4D 68-????? 3-6716 of the 32nd TFW, April 1981

5
F-4E 69-077?? 3-6570 of the 31st TFW, 21 July 1982

6
F-4E 71-01??? 3-6591 of the 11th TFW, September 1980

53

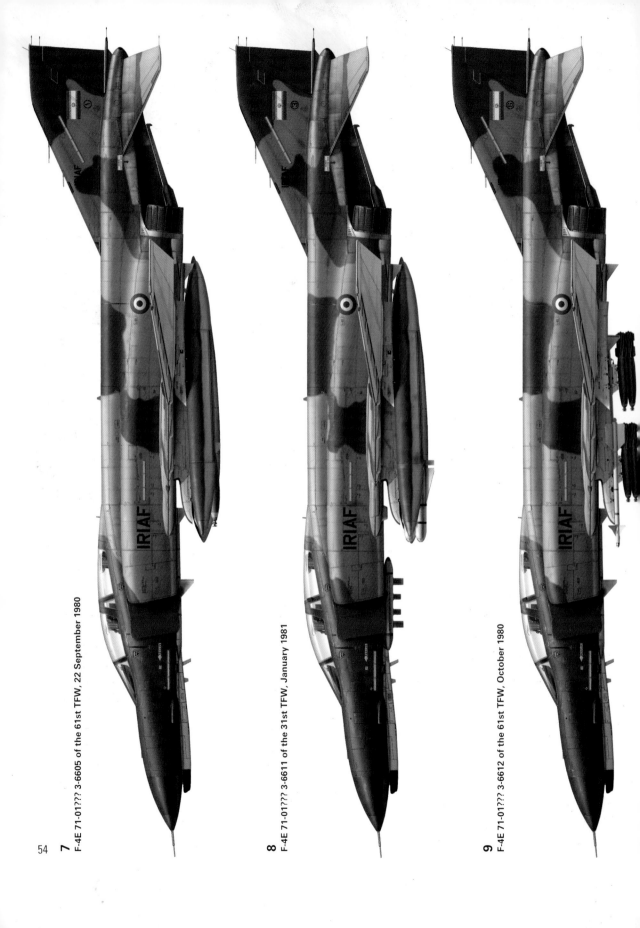

7
F-4E 71-01??? 3-6605 of the 61st TFW, 22 September 1980

8
F-4E 71-01??? 3-6611 of the 31st TFW, January 1981

9
F-4E 71-01??? 3-6612 of the 61st TFW, October 1980

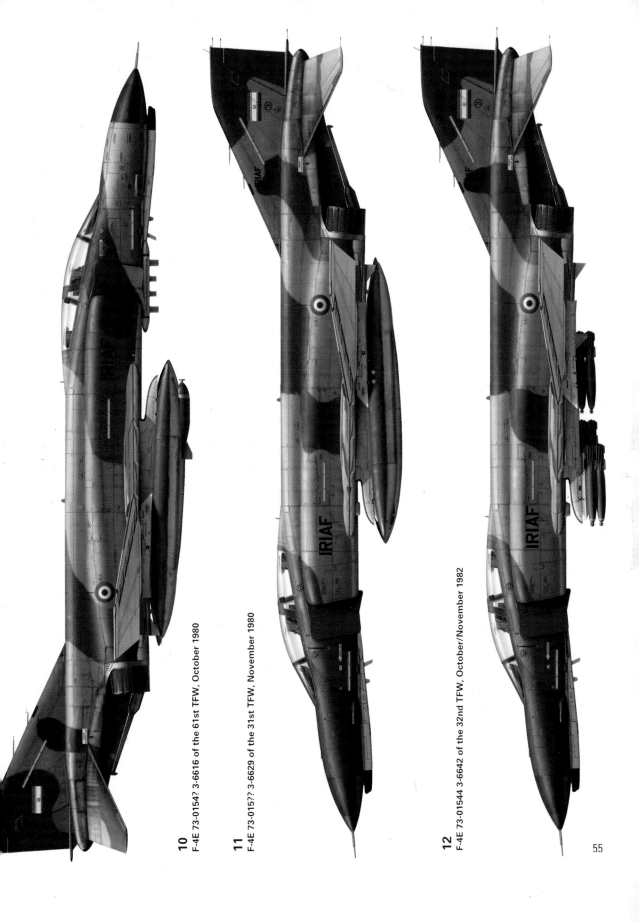

10
F-4E 73-0154? 3-6616 of the 61st TFW, October 1980

11
F-4E 73-0157? 3-6629 of the 31st TFW, November 1980

12
F-4E 73-0154 3-6642 of the 32nd TFW, October/November 1982

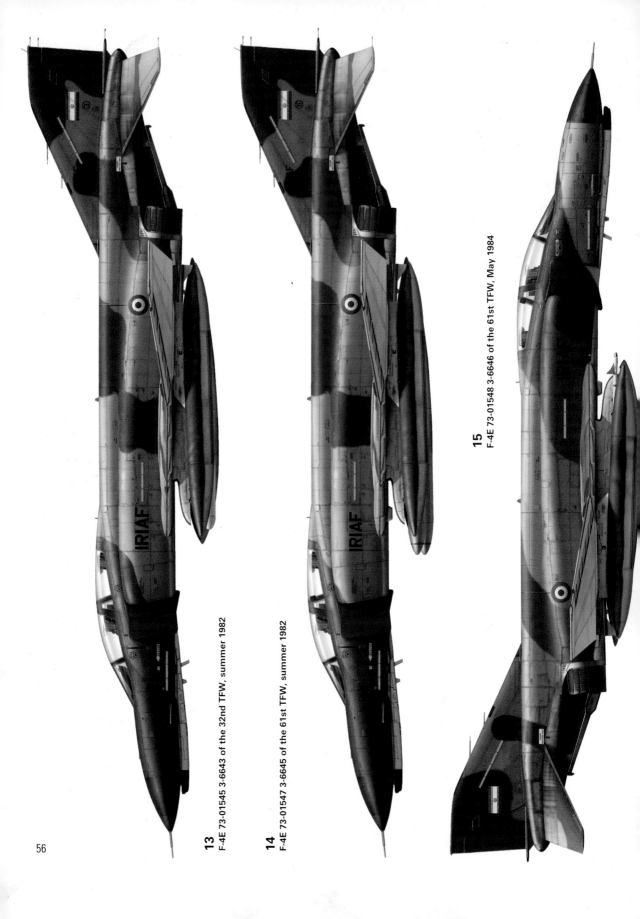

13
F-4E 73-01545 3-6643 of the 32nd TFW, summer 1982

14
F-4E 73-01547 3-6645 of the 61st TFW, summer 1982

15
F-4E 73-01548 3-6646 of the 61st TFW, May 1984

56

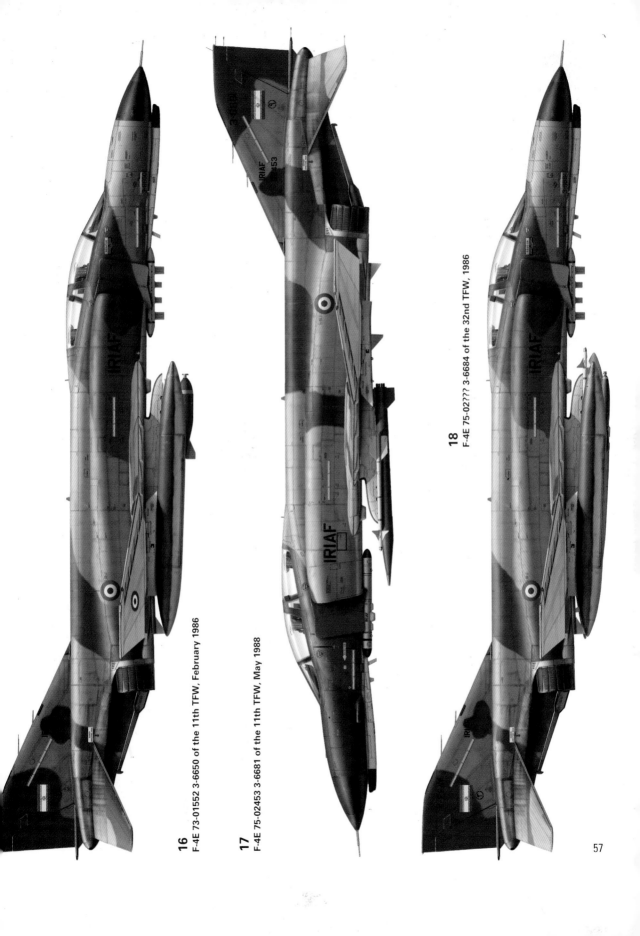

16
F-4E 73-01552 3-6650 of the 11th TFW, February 1986

17
F-4E 75-02453 3-6681 of the 11th TFW, May 1988

18
F-4E 75-02??? 3-6684 of the 32nd TFW, 1986

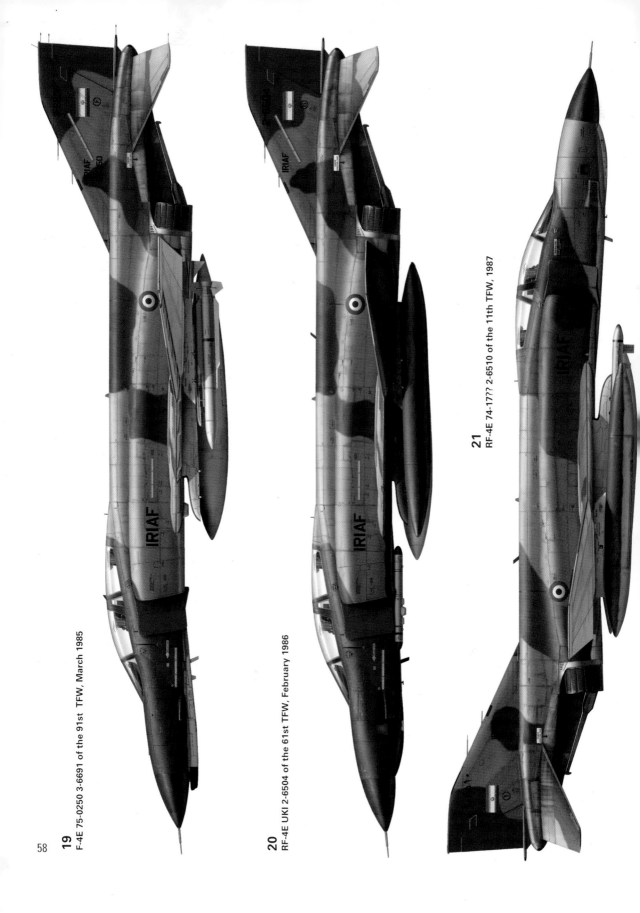

19
F-4E 75-0250 3-6691 of the 91st TFW, March 1985

20
RF-4E UKI 2-6504 of the 61st TFW, February 1986

21
RF-4E 74-17?? 2-6510 of the 11th TFW, 1987

58

22
Top view of a late-build F-4E Phantom II in standard IRIAF
three-shade camouflage

23
Underside view of a late-build F-4E Phantom II

1

2

3

4

5

6

7

8

9

10

11

12

sustained F-4 and F-5 strikes in less than 12 hours. By mid-April 1982, Iraqi forces were in such bad shape (the IrAF was left with barely 120 combat-ready aircraft) that Baghdad was ready to negotiate and even pull its troops out of Iran. Sensing victory, the Iranians launched Operation *Beit-ol-Moqaddass* on 30 April, which decimated Iraqi troops in Khuzestan and allowed the Iranian Army, and volunteers, to liberate Khoramshahr barely three weeks later.

During this period IRIAF Phantom IIs units also received a number of Israeli-supplied ECM pods, and crews also experimented with strike operations flown at high altitude. Such attacks rendered the F-4s immune to Iraqi SAMs, although these missions were then disrupted by IrAF interceptors such as the newly-delivered Mirage F 1EQ and MiG-25PD. These inflicted numerous losses on the Iranians.

The SAM and AAA threat remained constant throughout the war, as Maj Daryush 'Z' explained;

'We were flying against layered SAM defences, massed anti-aircraft guns and radar-guided anti-aircraft guns, as well as large groups of Iraqi interceptors, which were sometimes aggressively flown. Hardly anybody can understand what we were up against. Most people think that the Iraqi air defences were a joke, mainly because Iraqis are "Arabs". But they were no joke. Indeed, in the Baghdad area alone, they had over a thousand anti-aircraft weapons, including 100 mm guns, which were effective from ground level up to 22,750ft. These were the greatest threat we faced.

'Most IRIAF pilots became very good at distinguishing the type of anti-aircraft artillery the Iraqis were firing at them by the colour of the smoke from the shell bursts – white was 23 mm or 37 mm, blue was 57 mm and black with orange in the middle was 85 mm or 100 mm. One hit from any of these could cost us both our aeroplane and our lives. Any IRIAF pilot who tells you he didn't fear the Iraqi anti-aircraft artillery is a liar. During the war, I was twice forced to abort a mission against targets in the Baghdad area because the hostile AAA was so dense that to continue the mission would have been suicidal.

'The Iraqi SAMs could also be deadly. We thought they had "only" some 9000, but a captured IrAF pilot proudly told us that there were over 18,000 missiles in Iraq! In certain areas, Iraqi SAMs could be encountered

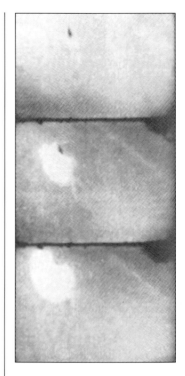

On 22 September 1981, two F-4Es that had been forward-deployed to TFB 4 were on a patrol over the southern front when two bomb-carrying Iraqi MiG-21MFs ventured into their area. Using their APX-80 'Combat Tree' enemy IFF interrogator equipment to full advantage, the Phantom II crews closed on the Iraqis without being detected and then opened fire. This MiG-21MF was torn apart by the explosion of its fuel tanks and bomb load (*authors' collection*)

In March 1982, during Operation *Fat'holmobin*, IRIAF Phantom IIs again used large numbers of Maverick missiles to decimate Iraqi armoured formations. In one instance, a complete Iraqi armoured division was destroyed in less than 12 hours. F-4E 3-6611 is seen here just prior to take off, the jet being armed with Sidewinders and Sparrows, as well as Mavericks (*authors' collection*)

at any altitude up to 65,000 ft, but below 300 ft, the Iraqis always had trouble tracking our fighters. Most Iraqi SAM kills against the IRIAF were achieved from behind, and the Iranian pilots never saw them until it was too late. There were three main tactics we used to out-smart Iraqi SAMs: we could execute a high-speed dive to below 330 ft and fly away at highest speed; we could lure the SAM into a dive and then pull up sharply; or we could pull several high-g turns. All these tactics were high-g, gut-wrenching manoeuvres, and the Iraqi SAMs could not usually match them if they were executed in time.'

Following the defeat at Khoramshahr, Baghdad ordered almost all Iraqi forces in Iran to pull back in the vain hope that this would result in Tehran assuming that the war was over, and therefore to stop the fighting. However, the Iranian clergy had other ideas.

COMBAT VETERANS

In the history of aerial warfare, it is rare to find pilots that have survived more than a thousand combat sorties against opponents as well-equipped and determined as the Iraqis over such a long period of time. They might complete two or even three tours of duty, and amass up to 400 or 450 combat sorties, but most of the Iranian Phantom II pilots who started flying when the war with Iraq began, and survived to the end, flew many more. In fact 1000 was not uncommon. So how did they manage to survive? Maj Daryush 'Z' explains;

'I survived not because I was the bravest, the most loyal or the smartest pilot in the IRIAF. I was none of these, but I was very lucky. I was lucky in that I was well trained to fly and fight when the Shah spared no expense in training Iranian pilots. This fact alone I feel allowed me to survive the long war years. For example, my earlier training paid off best during a raid that I took part in against a very important, and "large", fuel storage depot some six miles west of the major IrAF base at Kirkuk on 7 March 1982.

'My wingman and I pulled our Phantom IIs up to an altitude of 6500 ft over our target, before commencing our diving attack on a group of eight large fuel storage tanks. Needless to say, the area was well-defended by the Iraqis. As we released our bombs, my backseater called out a SAM warning as at least four French-made Roland missiles raced towards our Phantom IIs. Have just got rid of the weight and drag of my bombs, I instinctively pulled into a hard 5g+ turning dive from 5200 ft as two Roland missiles darted past my F-4. One or two other SAMs then hit my wingman's Phantom II, engulfing it in a bright orange fireball. As there was nothing I could do to help, I attempted to clear the target area as fast as possible. The Iraqis were not finished with me yet, however.

'I recall the sky being filled with columns of black smoke from the fires started by our bombs. Then, as new missile warning shrieks sounded in my headphones, I could see what seemed to be hundreds of SAM trails climbing up from the ground. My backseater warned me that an SA-3 had locked onto our Phantom II from the left, and was closing fast. I was only able to dodge it by turning into the missile at that precise moment at high speed, after which I dived to a lower altitude so as to hide in the ground clutter. Descending to just 200 ft, I levelled off and stayed at this height until we had reached the safety of the hills north-west of Kirkuk, where Iraqi radar could not track us.

This official photograph of a young 2Lt Abbas Dowran was taken shortly after his graduation from pilot training. Very early in his career, Dowran distinguished himself by flying Phantom IIs far beyond what was considered to be their maximum range. During the war with Iraq, he personally led at least 90 strikes deeper than 60 miles into enemy-held territory, and by June 1982 he had flown well over 2500 sorties, including more than 900 combat missions (*authors' collection*)

'Lt Javid, the young pilot who had been my wingman on this mission, was without a doubt an intelligent, brave and loyal IRIAF Phantom II pilot, but he died along with his WSO because he lacked training. Older, better-trained pilots flew the remaining two F-4s sortied on this mission, and they both returned intact. So it was our training – not how brave, loyal or smart we might have been – which counted most. We could not have survived any of our missions without the training we had received pre-war. My training had given me both the skills and the determination that I would draw on time and again during the war with Iraq.'

Sometimes, though, training, determination, skill, daring and all the other qualities possessed by modern combat pilots were not enough to guarantee their survival, as was the case with Lt Col Abbas Dowran.

In the late summer of 1982, Baghdad was to host the summit of non-aligned nations. The new National Conference Centre was built for the purpose near al-Mossana International Airport. Holding the summit in Baghdad was a matter of prestige for the Iraqi regime. It was also a major political blow to the Iranian leadership. IRIAF high command received a direct order from Ayatollah Khomeini himself, stating 'the summit must not be allowed to be held in Baghdad at any cost'. An operation was therefore planned to deliver a simple message – Iran can strike you at will.

The most experienced IRIAF commanders and pilots were selected to plan and carry out the strike, and it came as no surprise when Abbas Dowran was chosen to be mission leader. He had been one of the few pilots to advance in rank after the revolution, and had become the highly-respected deputy CO of TFB3. As a pilot, he had already flown several hundred combat sorties against Iraq. Capt H Assefi remembered;

'I know of no better Phantom II pilot than Lt Col Abbas Dowran, either before or after his death. Over the years, I have been lucky enough to fly with USAF, IDFAF and many IIAF/IRIAF F-4 pilots, and Lt Col Dowran had no equal, even though the Americans and Israelis were among the best. On strike missions into Iraq, regardless of whether it was day or night, he would fly his Phantom II lower and faster than anybody else, and frequently beyond the edge of its design limits. He would do this time and time again. Frequently, he came back from missions with his "g-meter" tripped, which meant that groundcrews had to check his F-4 for potential structural failures. Yet he always returned to tell the story.

'His marksmanship with the Phantom II's General Electric M-61A1 Vulcan gun was legendary, and he used it against the Iraqis without hesitation – although he took no personal delight in strafing Iraqi troops. Lt Col Dowran was also known for his high Maverick kill rate against Iraqi armour, especially when flying with his favourite WSO, Lt A Sharifi. Interestingly, and for reasons only known to themselves, when Dowran and Sharifi flew AGM-65 missions, their F-4 was usually armed with only two Mavericks, despite the capability of the LAU-88 launchers (one could be mounted under each wing of the F-4E) to carry three rounds apiece.

'Lt Col Dowran achieved only average delivery accuracy with iron bombs, however. Being wise enough to harbour no allusions about his capabilities, he adjusted his own tactics to counter this small weakness by using cluster weapons as often as possible. Such weapons were very popular with many IRIAF Phantom II pilots, myself included.

'As I said, Dowran was the best F-4 pilot in the IRIAF in my eyes, and in those of many other Iranian officers. Yet, in all honesty, his greatest value to the IRIAF was as a mission planner. Capable of executing well-conceived strikes on the enemy, this should have been Dowran's primary duty. From the very start of the war, he had been able to plan hard-hitting missions against strategic targets in Iraq using outdated intelligence from American and IIAF records, most of which was at least two to three years old. Using his own insight, along with good judgment, Dowran's non-traditional interdiction missions into Iraq were, according to IRIAF statistics, 90 per cent successful. They were also very, very costly for the Iraqis in terms of lives and equipment lost. Sadly, it did not take long before a number of captured IRIAF personnel told the Iraqis about Dowran, and he soon became the most wanted Iranian pilot.'

Dowran even survived several assassination plots, and Assefi explains why he was so highly respected in the IRIAF, and so feared in Iraq;

'In-flight refuelling was second nature to most IRIAF pilots by the start of the war, and Lt Col Dowran considered this to be one of our greatest advantages over the Iraqis when planning strategic missions against them. The Iraqis never completely understood how far we could reach, and they often felt themselves safe from our Phantom IIs. Lt Col Dowran always planned precise and survivable raids deep into the heart of Iraq, and we always seemed to take a route, and attack, from the directions least expected by the Iraqis. For entry into Iraq he especially liked to use the hilly terrain along the border, using paths that he had tested himself.

'Dowran was known to be most reluctant to ask others to do what he would not do himself. That earned him much respect among the pilots,

During his combat career, Dowran swiftly developed a predilection for British-made Hunting BL 755 cluster bombs (seen here on this soon to be refuelled F-4E), of which at least 3000 were supplied to Iran before the war. It proved to be a formidable weapon, and although up to three could be mounted under each wing of the F-4, usually not more than two would be carried to avoid creating excessive drag. On his last mission into Iraq, however, Dowran's Phantom II was armed with two Mk 84s, which were the only weapons considered heavy enough to cause significant damage to the target (*authors' collection*)

but also placed him in much danger. Using these paths, our air force penetrated Iraq's air defence zones almost with ease – indeed, some Iraqis thought we used magic! We even experienced few problems penetrating the most heavily defended area in the world – the Baghdad Air Defence Zone. But one should not think that flying missions into Iraq posed little threat to Iranian crews.

After entering enemy airspace, we still had to attack targets defended by SAMs, AAA and fighters. We then had to return home, which seemed harder every time, and was usually more risky than getting into Iraq. In most cases, we could rely on our ability to fly low and fast, outrunning the air defences.'

Such opinions about Abbas Dowran were widespread within the IRIAF, and he became a legend both during and after his lifetime. Not

Capt Dowran and Capt Alireza Yassini (right) were among the top Iranian Phantom II pilots. Together with men such as Maj Manuchehr Mohagheghi, Maj Asqar Sepidmooy-Azar and Capt Hossein Khalatbari, they virtually destroyed the Iraqi navy in October and November 1980, mostly with Maverick air-to-ground missiles (*authors' collection*)

surprisingly, he was considered the best at planning and executing missions aimed straight at the heart of Iraq.

Yet despite the anti-summit mission being of the utmost importance to the Iranian war effort, Dowran's last sortie remains controversial. Curiously, he had also been ordered to 'survey' Baghdad's western air defence network during the course of an already dangerous mission. Why he was told to do this remains unclear, for such a mission should have been entrusted to an RF-4E, which had the necessary equipment to photograph the area in question. It seems the Iranian leadership wanted Dowran to make a clear demonstration of the IRIAF's ability to operate undisturbed over Baghdad itself. Clearly it was a risky, almost suicidal undertaking. Capt Assefi has his own theory about this part of the order;

'Following the outbreak of war with Iraq, Lt Col Dowran quickly became a hero to the IRIAF, despite his modest demeanour. It was also well-known to the Iranian government that he was popular with the general public, especially in his home town of Shiraz. Being a hero in Iran brought its own risks, as heroes can easily gain power over the masses. Clearly, no living hero in Iran could be allowed to have power beyond the clerics' wishes – especially as our clerics did not trust the "Shah's pilots", which we all were. Lt Col Dowran ran into problems with the IRIAF headquarters and "others" soon after the war started because he spoke out against the treatment of so many of the air force's best pilots and officers.

'He also had a problem with the way the Iranian government was handling the war with Iraq. He wanted Iran to stage one all-out drive into Iraq, taking Baghdad by force no matter what the cost – and thus end the conflict. Dowran's plan called for the IRIAF to be at full strength for this drive, giving air cover and support to the Iranian Army and Guards in their all-out drive to take Baghdad. He was sure his plan could end the war within days, leaving Iran the clear victor. The government and other decision-makers were not interested, but I felt at that time that once Dowran's plan had been seen in certain circles, he was a marked man.'

At noon on Wednesday 21 July 1982, three IRIAF F-4Es, each armed with two Mk 84 bombs, two Sparrow missiles and one ECM pod, took off from Nojeh on the top-secret mission to destroy Baghdad's National Conference Centre. The two Phantom IIs scheduled to attack the Iraqi capital were flown by Dowran, with Capt Mansour Kazemiyan as his WSO, and Maj Mahmoud Eskandari, with his WSO being 2Lt Nasser Bagheri. The third Phantom II, crewed by Maj Tirdad and Capt Oqba'i, was to be held in reserve.

The three jets were supported by two Phoenix-armed F-14As and a single Boeing 707-3J9C 'Roving Eye' tanker/pathfinder, which were to escort the Phantom IIs to the border town of Mandali, where they would await their return. Capt Havee 'N' explained how the drama unfolded;

'While the two Phantom IIs that were to fly the mission were being refuelled by the tanker, the spare F-4E left the formation and flew a diversionary manoeuvre over Naft-Shahr, further to the north. Once the Iraqi air defences started tracking it, Lt Col Dowran and Maj Eskandari descended to low level and thundered towards Baghdad. But they fell into a well-laid trap – the IrAF/ADC had deployed several Euromissile Roland 2 all-weather SAM sites in and around the city to defend the most important installations, and cover the most likely approach routes of our F-4s. Two mobile Roland 2 sites were positioned on the outskirts of Baghdad.

'These weapons, with a maximum engagement range of just four miles, were mounted on an armoured truck chassis and emplaced on earth mounds to give them a clear field of view. Additionally, the IrAF/ADC deployed several static Roland 2 SAM sites on the rooftops of high-rise buildings to improve low-level coverage. Our RWR systems were not programmed to recognise such a threat.

'The first F-4E, IRIAF serial 3-6570, flown by Dowran, was hit as soon as it came within range of a Roland 2 SAM site, and before the crew could react. Kazemiyan ejected and was taken prisoner, but Dowran remained in his crippled aircraft and almost certainly crashed it into the control tower at al-Mossana airport. Being the key IRIAF planner, and therefore knowing too much, he obviously chose to die, rather than to be captured and risk interrogation under torture. The total damage inflicted by his aircraft and bombs was reported to have been "a hotel and the taxiway of the airport", but al-Mossana was closed to civilian traffic for the first time since October 1980. Capt Kazemiyan was released by the Iraqis in 1990, following the invasion of Kuwait.'

In the remaining F-4E, Eskandari was forced to jettison his bombs to

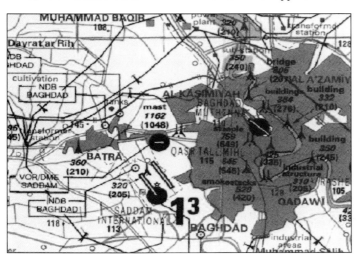

A navigational map of central Baghdad, showing the position of al-Mossana airport (called Muthenna here). The actual target of Dowran's last raid was the National Congress Centre, which is sited just a few kilometres to the south-east, in the centre of the city. Dowran planned to approach the target from the opposite direction to that expected, but his plan went disastrously awry because his Phantom II was shot down by Iraqi Roland 2 SAMs (*NIMA Tactical Pilotage Chart 1:500,000 scale*)

evade SAMs. Turning for home, he had just engaged the afterburners when a 57 mm flak round exploded near his cockpit, spraying it with shrapnel. Two formations of Iraqi interceptors then scrambled in an effort to catch him.

Recognising the serious nature of the threat facing the surviving F-4, the leader of the F-14 patrol disobeyed his orders not to enter Iraqi airspace. Accelerating to give his weapons a longer reach and higher energy, he fired a single AIM-54A from a range of 65 miles against a formation of four MiG-23s which was closing on the Phantom II from the north. The missile hit the lead MiG-23, blotting it out in a huge explosion which also downed a second 'Flogger'.

Meanwhile, the F-14 leader's wingman joined the fray, engaging a section of four Su-22s and shooting one down with another AIM-54 that was fired from a distance of 22 miles. The crippled F-4 was then able to leave Iraq and refuel from the tanker, before recovering to its base.

This reconnaissance photograph of the military area of Saddam International Airport was taken by an IRIAF RF-4E in the early stages of the war. The aircraft visible in their revetments are, from left to right, a Mil Mi-8 'Hip' helicopter, a MiG-21 'Fishbed' and two Su-7 'Fitters'. Note the numerous entrances to the underground facilities at the top pf the photo. It is very likely that the air defences positioned around numerous installations on the northern side of the airport were responsible for shooting down Dowran's F-4E (authors' *collection*)

MESSAGE DELIVERED

In tactical terms, therefore, Dowran's last mission was only partially successful. But the intended message had been delivered, despite the Phantom IIs failing to fly undisturbed over Baghdad and bomb their target. The raid did cause some damage, however. The resulting chaos could not be concealed, and reports of Iranian Phantom IIs 'bombing' Baghdad appeared in the international press. The non-aligned summit was re-located to India, where it was held in February 1983. The operation

The crews of the two F-14As which covered Dowran's last raid into Iraq had been ordered to remain on the Iranian side of the border, but when the F-4E flown by Dowran's wingman, Maj Mahmoud Eskandari – which had been damaged by a 57 mm shell hit near the cockpit – was almost cut off by two flights of Iraqi interceptors, the Tomcat pilots could not hold back. Disobeying their orders, they raced into Iraq and shot down three fighters with two AIM-54s fired from more than 50 miles away (*authors' collection*)

therefore became – just like several earlier raids – a perfect example of a well-publicised attack against politically-sensitive targets of great propaganda value. Other results of the operation remain controversial.

For one thing, the mission's target represented a departure from IRIAF policy of avoiding civilian casualties wherever possible. Tehran was swift to put up a smokescreen by claiming that the actual target had been the ad-Dowrah oil refinery in southern Baghdad. Careful research of Iraqi documents revealed that they believed the attack had missed its objective. But in one instance the domestic press claimed that the Iranians had destroyed a hotel full of civilians, including foreigners, prior to Dowran's F-4 being shot down. No confirmation for such a claim was ever found, not even in the Iraqi media. This seems odd, because at the time the Iraqis would have exploited any civilian casualties for propaganda purposes.

The actual events contrast markedly with the official Iraqi line. Despite being stunned by the attack – again, there had been no advance warning – the Iraqi authorities were in fact swift to use the operation, and Dowran's death, to cover up a terrorist attack staged by a Shiite opposition group on a government building in the centre of Baghdad several hours after the Iranian raid. A bomb planted outside the building gutted all six floors, killing and injuring an unknown number of people. All the injured were removed from the city for treatment. The Iraqi authorities recovered an unexploded Mk 84 bomb and took it 4.5 miles to the destroyed building, where it was put on display.

Many Iraqi reports make it clear that al-Mossana International airport was indeed closed to civilian traffic after an Iranian attack that day. Most of the reports indicate that one of the Iranian aircraft penetrated the airport defences – some of the heaviest in the whole of Iraq – while the other was shot down. Other contemporary reports indicate that a number of Western embassies asked their governments for permission to evacuate their nationals from Iraq other than by air. Based on these two facts alone, two conclusions can be reached. Firstly, al-Mossana was indeed damaged by the Iranian Phantom IIs which broke through its defences on 21 June 1982. And secondly, Lt Col Dowran was an excellent planner and exceptionally skilled pilot, for he would not otherwise have been able to get two F-4Es to the target area in the first place.

Once they realised who they had shot down, the Iraqis changed their tactics and started to celebrate the loss of a top Iranian pilot. Iraqi Army Gen Maher Abdul-Rashid claimed the 'bandit Dowran purposely attacked an Iraqi civilian target' (which had an anti-aircraft gun on the roof), and that this showed the 'uncivilised and barbaric' nature of Khomeini's Iran. The Iraqis were pleased to have killed Dowran. On 4 August 1982, US intelligence intercepted a message sent from the Iraqi Ministry of Information to the Iraqi embassy in Cairo, which stated;

'As the "Fetr" festivities end, we share this joyous news. Now let it be known that our brave Baghdad defence forces have taken the life of Iranian bandit pilot Abbas Dowran during the Iranian raid on our capital on Wednesday 21 July.'

The Iranian authorities were slow to inform the IRIAF and the Iranian public about the death of such a well-known and highly respected war hero. Most IRIAF pilots only learned about his death weeks later. Iraq returned Dowran's remains to Iran on 21 July 2002.

TO THE BITTER END

It was late in 1982 that the Iranians received their first indication that the war with Iraq would be a long one. But that was still some time away when, in mid-July 1982, after the first offensive by the Islamic Revolutionary Guards Corps (IRGC) into Iraq had been swiftly stopped by the defenders of Basrah, the regular Iranian army prepared two smaller operations for the autumn. Both were undertaken on the northern sectors of the front. The first, codenamed *Muslim-Ibn-Aqil*, began on 1 October, and the second, *Moharram*, followed on 6 November. Despite some limited gains, both operations ground to a halt in the Iraqi defensive lines. Bad weather then intervened, and the offensive developed into a series of air-to-ground battles in which aircraft and helicopters were used intensively.

During this period the Iraqis claimed more than 30 Iranian fighters and helicopters shot down, most of which were Phantom IIs (including one F-4 'shot down' by an Mi-24 helicopter!) and Tomcats. Actual IRIAF losses amounted to just one F-4E downed by a MiG-21 during a raid on Rashid air base, two F-5Es and a pair of AH-1Js over the front. In reality, the Iranians had inflicted heavy losses on the IrAF, with TFB 3 Phantom IIs flying strikes on Iraqi airfields, followed by attacks on ground troops. A MiG-23 and an Su-22 were also shot down during the latter missions.

In December came the defection of an Iraqi MiG-23MS pilot, who brought with him some disquieting news. An F-4E from TFB 4 was

During the successful 1982 offensives, Iranian troops liberated Khoramshahr, this city subsequently being dubbed the 'Iranian Stalingrad' because it had been completely destroyed in the fierce fighting to secure its freedom. In the wake of the liberation, the wreckage of an F-4E was found amongst the ruins. It is thought to have been the aircraft flown by Capt Azizollah Jafari and 1Lt Mohamad-Reza Karami from TFB 6, which had been shot down on 27 September 1980 (*authors' collection*)

The 1982 summer offensives saw Iranian ground forces launch a series of incursions into enemy territory aimed primarily at capturing Iraq's second-largest city, Basrah. The first two attacks were stopped mainly by Iraqi Army Aviation Corps' counter attacks using helicopter gunships such as this Mi-25 'Hind', seen here flying over Iraqi mechanised troops in the Shalamcheh area. Although large and not particularly manoeuvrable, the 'Hinds' proved highly effective, although contrary to press reports at the time, they did not shoot down any Iranian F-4s (*US DoD*)

IRIAF Phantom IIs flew innumerable strikes along the frontline against Iraqi troops, mainly targeting motor pools and supply bases. In this case, the rearward-facing strike-camera mounted beneath a low-flying F-4E has recorded a strafing attack made against army tankers at a fuel depot. Note the shadow of the attacking Phantom II, demonstrating just how close to the ground pilots flew in order to deliver their attacks with as much precision as possible (*authors' collection*)

involved in the incident, as Maj Daryush 'Z' explains;

'On 2 December 1982, four IrAF MiG-23s of the 84th FS were attacking Iranian positions south of Vahdati air base. Four F-4Es and F-5Es were scrambled to intercept them. Closing on the jets, one of the Phantom II pilots picked out a MiG which was flying high and slow. Coming closer, the Iranian saw to his surprise that the MiG was lowering its landing gear and turning on its navigation lights. The Phantom II pilot rolled out and positioned himself beside the Iraqi, who appeared to be waving to the Iranians. The situation was reported to Vahdati GCI, which was obviously taken by surprise and assumed this was some kind of Iraqi trick. But the Phantom II pilot assured them that his counterpart in the MiG wanted to follow him back to base. So a decision was taken to advise the F-4 pilot to lead the MiG-23MS in for a landing, but also to shoot it down at once if the Iraqi tried to retract his gear.

'The MiG landed without incident. The pilot stopped his aircraft where he was ordered, climbed out of the cockpit and handed his sidearm to Iranian personnel, who were now inspecting the IRIAF's newest addition. The Iraqi lieutenant was first brought to base headquarters and, after two or three hours, was taken back to his aeroplane, where some photos were taken of him. Afterwards, the pilot was put into a C-130 transport and flown to TFB 1 for debriefing. During the interrogation in Tehran, the Iraqi said he was a member of the 84th Sqn, based at Tallil air base. However, he said that for this attack he had started from one of the Iraqi "super bases", codenamed 202E, north-east of Tallil. We were unaware of the existence of such bases, and were astonished to here the Iraqi pilot talk of heavily hardened aircraft shelters built in Iraq by the Yugoslavs.'

While the report that the Yugoslavs were building heavily fortified air bases in Iraq was fascinating, the other intelligence gleaned from the Iraqi pilot proved horrifying for the Iranian regime. It was discovered that the IrAF, so successfully contained during the 1982 offensives, and barely

During the second half of 1982, the Iranian Army engaged the Iraqis in two offensives which threatened to breach the front only 75 miles east of Baghdad. F-4Es from the 31st and 32nd TFWs, based at Nojeh, flew a series of highly effective strikes in which they repeatedly hit Iraqi armour with British and US-supplied CBUs and napalm. This Phantom II (3-6629), carrying four BL 755s, was photographed from a Boeing 707-3J9C tanker moments after refuelling. Minutes later it headed into Iraq in search of its target (*authors' collection*)

This MiG-23MS of the IrAF's 84th Sqn was flown to Vahdati air base by a defecting Iraqi pilot on 2 December 1982. The Iranians made little effort to hide their new acquisition, and the aircraft was subsequently destroyed in an Iraqi strike just hours after it had arrived. This unique still was taken from a video that had been shot of the MiG moments after it had landed in Iran (*authors' collection*)

able to conduct any kind of offensive operations, had ordered over 100 new combat aircraft from the USSR. These were now arriving, making it clear that the war would last far longer than had been anticipated.

There was an ironic consequence to the defection, as Maj Daryush 'Z' recalls;

'As for the fate of the MiG-23MS, in their wisdom IRIAF personnel left it in the open on the ramp, barely 30 yards from two empty hardened aircraft shelters! Six or seven hours later the IrAF attacked Vahdati again with two groups of four Su-22s, and they found the missing MiG. Needless to say, it did not survive the attack.'

By 1983 spare parts had begun to reach IRIAF units far more regularly thanks to the repair of logistical systems computers. The contents of several huge underground parts stockpiles were also released. At the same time the US government rubber stamped the export of several large spares shipments to Iran.

Tactically, the IRIAF also began to raise its game, and in January a programme to improve the co-ordination between interceptors and SAMs was initiated. This was done primarily to counter the increasing number of hit and run attacks being made by Iraqi fighter-bombers on Iranian border cities. Through the rapid creation of 'killing zones' in Khuzestan, Ilam and Kermanshah provinces by the end of February 1983, the IRIAF was able to shoot down some 25 Iraqi aircraft, including several that fell to F-4Es. The IRIAF also made effective use of new ECM pods supplied by Israel. Time and again the IrAF was forced to abandon offensives and concentrate on defending its own airfields and oil installations.

Maj Daryush 'Z' recounts his experiences from this period;

'The Iraqi air defences depended on a large number of very modern

From late 1982 through to the early spring of 1983, IRIAF RF-4Es were kept active searching out targets in preparation for the Iranian spring offensives. Here, an RF-4E flies over an Iraqi SA-2 site, which has responded by ripple-firing three missiles. None came near the Phantom II, however (*authors' collection*)

An IRIAF RF-4E thunders along a mountain valley in northern Iran. Reconnaissance pilots became expert at low-flying their Phantom IIs, sometimes operating so low that on their return to base they would find tree branches hanging from underwing pylons. The ability to fly in such a way was not just a matter of personal pride for Iranian pilots – it was the only way to guarantee their survival (*authors' collection*)

Sometimes IRIAF RF-4Es had to fly at high level in Iraq, relying on speed as their only form of defence. Intercepting the fast, high-flying RF-4E proved exceptionally difficult for Iraqi fighters, which were only occasionally successful. In this case, the Iraqi pilot was too eager, overshooting the recce-Phantom II, whose cameras recorded this picture of a Mirage F 1EQ in planform (*authors' collection*)

ground radars, with hardened control centres that were later integrated into a French-designed air defence system called *Kari*. It had 300 complete radar detection sets, and was a first-class system even by today's standards. Frequently, the Iraqis didn't use their SAM systems' surveillance radars, but only the fire-control radars, and only then at the last moment. The reason was that our Radar Homing And Warning System (RHAWS) could detect their radars and alert us that we were being tracked. There was a shrill sound in our headphones, and the approximate bearing and radar type were displayed on a small screen in the rear cockpit.

'Sometimes the Iraqis would try to trick us by firing their SAMs blindly without any guidance when they knew we were in the area, hoping that some missiles would pass close enough to us to activate their proximity fuses. During one of my missions in 1983 I encountered just such a trap, and I must say it took me by surprise, as the only warning I got that a SAM had been fired was the bright glow from its motor!'

For the rest of 1983 the IRGC, supported by the army, launched one offensive into Iraq after another, but each was halted after minimal gains. Usually, the regular armed forces and the IRGC were reluctant to help each other in such operations unless the situation became desperate, such as during the fierce counterattacks by the IrAF on IRGC ranks. Most calls were immediately answered by the IRIAF, which tended to deploy US-supplied MIM-23 SAMs in combination with interceptors. However, these efforts – even if highly successful at times – usually came too late to save the IRGC offensives.

From the summer of 1983, the Iraqis increased their efforts to interdict the shipping lanes along the Iranian Persian Gulf coast, while simultaneously attacking deeper into Iran. Initially, these operations were sporadic and lacked precision, but they nevertheless put the IRIAF under pressure, as the air force had to spread its assets thinly along the whole battle front.

The limited number of published reports detailing the air war between Iraq and Iran usually state that 1984 was a very bad year for the IRIAF because of defections, general unrest and a growing lack of spares. Much of these 'facts' are based on complete misunderstandings, however. Western observers often failed to comprehend the real situation because they lacked up to date information on the operations of the air force at that time. In fact, the IRIAF remained fully operational throughout 1984, flying at least 100 combat sorties per day on average. The F-4s, in particular, would often be held in the air for hours on end, patrolling with the support of multiple aerial refuellings from tankers. Such missions were common during major Iranian offensives, as Maj Daryush 'Z' complained;

'All those who say the IRIAF was not operational in 1984 should have said so to the commander-in-chief of the air force. We were flying as intensively as possible.'

This photograph, taken during a low-level RF-4E mission deep into Iraq, shows an SA-3 'Goa' (S-125 Pechora) SAM site, and its associated 'Low Blow' target tracking/fire-control radar (centre right). A P-15 'Flat Face' surveillance and target acquisition radar can also be seen in the top right corner of the shot. Note that all the launchers are turned away from the Phantom II (whose shadow can be seen in the lower right hand corner of the photo), which was an obvious sign that the Iraqi air defences had been taken by surprise once again (*authors' collection*)

So intensively, in fact, that there was not enough time to maintain the declining number of combat aircraft available. The complex F-4s suffered from a lack of anything beyond squadron-level maintenance, and even the IRAN (inspect and repair as necessary) procedure could not be completed to schedule. This inevitably caused many problems for IRIAF pilots, as they began to encounter an increasing number of main systems failures during combat operations. In January 1984, just such a failure almost claimed the life of Maj Golchin, CO of TFB3, his aircraft suffering a series of mechanical failures during a combat sortie deep into Iraq. Despite the presence of Iraqi interceptors, Golchin managed to nurse his Phantom II back across the border so that he and his WSO could eject safely. Subsequent research has confirmed that the lost Phantom II had exceeded all its servicing schedules, and was known to be prone to mechanical failures.

Iranian tactics also changed at this time, as Maj Daryush 'Z' explained;

'From 1984, we attacked in pairs, and almost never more than two pairs per mission. This was not so much due to a shortage of aeroplanes, but mainly because the Iraqi air defences improved to the point where sending larger groups of IRIAF jets on missions only red flagged them to

From the summer of 1982, the IrAAC (instructed by East German pilots) started deploying 'hunter-killer' teams of Mi-25 and SA 342 Gazelle helicopters, which inflicted numerous losses on Iranian ground units. The IRIAF hit back, and on 16 June 1983, Lt Col Siavash Bayani, flying an F-4E, shot down an Mi-25, flown by East German pilot Maj Ralph Geschke, near Kut. This AT-2-armed 'Hind' survived the war, only to be captured by US forces in February 1991 during Operation *Desert Storm* (*US DoD*)

Time and again during 1983, IrAF air defences managed to shoot down Phantom IIs deep inside Iraq. This F-4E was hit by Iraqi SAMs early that year, the jet crashing somewhere in the south of the country. The Iraqis recovered an ALQ-87 ECM pod from the wreckage and duly passed it on to the Soviets (*authors' collection*)

the Iraqis. These later IRIAF missions were almost always hit-and-run attacks. Often they were mounted just to let the Iraqis know we were still able to hurt them. IRIAF HQ had no real strategic plan against the Iraqis other then to try and hold them at bay. In contrast to our random, erratic and even half-hearted efforts, the Iraqis, on the other hand, had a long term strategic plan. They were happy to steadily chip away at Iran's ability to make war against them, which they did until the end.'

LONE HUNTERS

In October 1983 France initiated Operation *Sugar*, which saw five Dassault Super Etendards loaned to Iraq. These aircraft were then used in the so-called 'tanker war,' flying anti-shipping attacks deep into the Persian Gulf. Such attacks were not new, however, as the Iraqis had been using AM 39 Exocet-armed Super Frelons in this role since the late summer of 1981. The Iranians were swift to hunt the Super Etendards down on the rare occasions that the low-flying aircraft were detected, and by the summer of 1984 IRIAF Phantom II and Tomcat crews had claimed two jets confirmed destroyed and one probably destroyed (*Dassault Aviation via the authors*)

Despite these technical problems, the IRIAF continued to find effective employment for its F-4s. Here, Capt Ra'ssi 'A' and Maj Daryush 'Z' describe one of their successful missions during the spring of 1984;

'We had known since October 1983 that the IrAF had been loaned five French-made Super Etendards by their French friends. These aircraft, armed with the 150 AM 39 Exocet missiles that were already in the Iraqi arsenal, formed the 90th Sqn – the IrAF's first dedicated fixed wing anti-ship unit. In the IRIAF, we once again felt that the French were punishing us for buying only American-made fighters during the 1960s and 1970s. With Iraq having ordered over \$12bn worth of arms from France since the mid-1970s, we knew the French were Iraqi supporters at heart.'

Although the Super Etendards were delivered during October 1983 (as part of Operation *Sugar*), it was not until the end of March 1984 that the IrAF began using them effectively. This delay was caused by problems that beset the pilot conversion programme onto the new aircraft, and its weapons system. Once the small Super Etendard unit became operational,

Baghdad was swift to proclaim an 'aerial siege' of Khark Island. From March 1984, the Iraqis began sending their newest fighters to hunt for targets. Ra'ssi 'A' and Daryush 'Z' recalled;

'Once the Iraqi pilots began operational missions over the Persian Gulf, we soon learned their tactics. They would usually fly alone and mostly at lower attitudes, only occasionally climbing to higher attitudes in the hope of spotting a tanker. They would then return to lower altitudes. If an Iraqi Super Etendard located a target on its radar scope, it would only close in close enough to programme the Exocet missile and then fire it. We learned to take the AM 39 missile seriously, as very early on in the war an Iraqi Super Frelon helicopter had sunk one of our *Bayandor* class corvettes using an Exocet, killing many of the crew.

'These lone Iraqi hunters would soon find out that they were not always alone, and that even though the IrAF often made hit-and-run raids in the Persian Gulf, it was the IRIAF which controlled the airspace. They therefore started to use the Saudi-declared "Fahad Line" over the Persian Gulf as a safe haven, claiming that any IRIAF aeroplane which crossed that line would be considered hostile, and would be intercepted by their fighters. That was a big Arabic joke – we crossed the Fahad Line at will, and the Saudis did very little about it.

'For their part, the Iraqis declared their "warning zone" in the Gulf. That was a big Iraqi joke, as they had no control over the area, and it was actually the Iranian air force and navy which went where they wished in this "Iraqi" zone. With the Iranian navy controlling most of the northern Gulf and the US Navy controlling the remaining Gulf waters, the situation was clear, and there were no confrontations. The warships of the other nations based in the Gulf, including those of the Arab navies, had no real power, nor could they reasonably defend themselves.'

Capt Ra'ssi 'A' recalled one particular missions he flew;

'In April 1984 I was based at Bushehr (TFB 6) with the 62nd FS, flying F-4Es in the defence of Khark Island. At that time the IrAF was attacking many cities all over Iran. Tehran, in particular, was receiving an average of two air raids a day. Many of our fighters were being sent north to defend the cities, although they usually proved to be too few in number, too late and spread too thinly to offer any real opposition to the attacking Iraqi aircraft. This movement of aircraft north meant that we had only a few fighters available at TFB 6 – three or four F-4Es, a lone F-4D and one or two F-14As. These were occasionally based at Bushehr to escort our tankers and defend Khark.

'Thanks to a stroke of luck, on 2 April 1984 one of our Vickers-built *Saam*-class frigates, patrolling in the waters off Faw, detected a lone Iraqi aeroplane heading out over the Gulf after taking off from Um Qassr, near the Kuwaiti border, or from Shoaibah air base, some five miles from Basrah. The Iraqi jet had painted the Iranian frigate with its radar for a brief time, but its pilot did not appear to have the stomach

In 1983-84, F-4 crews were increasingly called upon to fly combat air patrols over the northern Persian Gulf. Sometimes, units would be held on standing alert, with crews strapped into their jets, at Bushehr and Omidiyeh so that they could react swiftly to any Iraqi attack. Although the Phantom II proved highly capable as an interceptor, the IRIAF experienced major problems detecting low-flying Iraqi fighters, which stayed in Iranian airspace just long enough to launch their weapons before IRIAF interceptors could be scrambled. The crew of this F-4E (3-6674) await the order to scramble at Bushehr, their boredom being punctuated by the arrival of a lone F-5E in the background. They have their canopies cranked open in an effort to keep cool, as the cockpit temperature in the hot Iranian sun could sometimes soar to 80°C during the summer months (*authors' collection*)

to take on an Iranian warship, and he continued flying south into the Persian Gulf. Our frigate radioed the flight path of the Iraqi fighter to the ground command and control station at Bushehr, which in turn scrambled our two alert F-4s. Judging from the information sent by our frigate, the enemy pilot was undoubtedly heading for the Khark area.

'We climbed to 9750 ft and split up, adopting a combat spread of 7.5 miles in order to cover as much of the Persian Gulf as possible. Despite having some idea of where the IrAF aircraft was heading, I felt the odds of tracking down the lone fighter were slim. From what little information our frigate had been able to pass to the control centre at Bushehr, I was betting that it was a Super Etendard with an Exocet missile under its wing, seeking a tanker to fire it at. Being a French fighter, it would be harder to track as our radar warning and IFF detecting gear was primarily configured to interrogate Russian aircraft radar frequencies and IFF – they hadn't been programmed by the Americans for French frequencies and IFF. However, our Phantom II radars were very good, as were our eyes, so I still had hopes of finding the lone Iraqi.

'We had just passed the Khark Defence Zone in our hunt when, some 75 miles from Faw, my wingman picked up a lone Iraqi fighter-bomber flying at just over 190 mph at a height of about 5200 ft. Just as we located the Iraqi jet, its pilot also detected us, and he commenced a hard turn towards the Kuwaiti or Saudi Arabian coast. I ordered my wingman to join up with my Phantom II as I turned to give chase. The Iraqi aeroplane was flying very slowly, so I now knew that we had indeed tracked down a heavily-loaded IrAF Super Etendard, and not a Mirage F 1. I accelerated to full power for about 20 seconds in order to get within missile range of the Iraqi. The enemy pilot continued to descend to a lower altitude, all the while flying west at what I'm sure was his best speed. We soon had radar lock, and I fired the first of two Sparrows at the Super Etendard as we closed on the Saudi coastline.

'The Iraqi aeroplane dived as we fired our missiles, and we spotted four more targets come up on our radar. It appeared that the Royal Saudi Air Force (RSAF), equipped with newly-supplied F-15s and guided by USAF AWACS, were heading out from their bases to meet us. The AWACS aircraft called us by radio, asking us in English to identify ourselves, and to state our intentions. "The hell with that", I thought.

Despite suffering losses to IRIAF fighters, Iraqi anti-shipping strikes intensified in April-May 1984, when all international traffic south of Khark was targeted. Phantom IIs from the 61st TFW could not prevent ships from being hit, as is graphically shown by this photograph of the tanker *al-Lahood*, which was wrecked by an Exocet missile on 7 May with the loss of one crew member (*authors' collection*)

Our intentions were clear. We didn't respond to the radio call, as our Sparrows appeared to have hit the Iraqi Super Etendard, causing it to disappear from our radar screens. We never responded to any of those radio calls.

'We then turned back to Iran, with the RSAF fighters staying some six miles behind our flight. We had no fuel left to engage them after the long pursuit, and my wing-man was experiencing radar prob-lems, so I was pleased the Saudis did not press us to engage them. We safely recovered to TFB 6. Further sorties against the IrAF's Exocet-armed "lone hunters" would be flown over the Persian Gulf.'

Indeed, IRIAF Phantom IIs were to regularly intercept Iraqi fighters as they searched for tankers along the Iranian coast, forcing dozens of them to drop their precious Exocet missiles. And, interestingly, while many publications about the air war between Iraq and Iran were reporting that barely any Iranian F-4s remained flyable, non-published assessments reserved for US political and military leaders did not concur with this view. Only a day after Ra'ssi 'A' and his wingman had intercepted the Super Etendard, the USAF and McDonnell Douglas issued a special report (46749-MH1984) to the Pentagon on the state of Iranian forces. Among other things, it stated;

'As to when the Iranian air force will lose its ability to maintain, utilise in combat and repair their F-4 Phantom II fleet, all experts now predict it will not lose this ability any time in the near future as Iran has made remarkably effective use of its Phantom II fleet. This is due in no small part to the inherent robustness of the Phantom II, and to Iranian air force technicians showing great ingenuity in husbanding their spare part stocks that were on hand before the war, and those spare parts covertly supplied during 1983 by the United States government. It should also be noted that the Iranian air force is also showing a hence-unknown ability to return battle-damaged F-4 Phantom IIs back to service.'

PHANTOM IIs ON THE PROWL

For the rest of 1984 and much of 1985, IRIAF Phantom IIs remained active over the Persian Gulf, mainly escorting convoys of Iranian tankers to Khark and Iranian ports in the northern Gulf. In response to intensive Iraqi anti-shipping strikes, the IRIAF started operations in May 1984 against ships bound for Kuwait and Saudi Arabia. This offensive saw F-4Es from TFB 6 engaging not only Iraqi but also Saudi fighters. Early clashes between the IRIAF and the RSAF were limited to 'shadow boxing', but the first air-to-air missiles were launched soon enough when, on 5 June, two Saudi F-15s intercepted a pair of Phantom IIs from Bushehr, downing one and killing its crew.

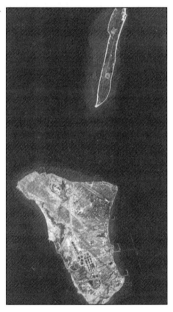

This satellite photograph of Khark shows the main island, with its oil installations and two tanker jetties, as well as the smaller island on which a MIM-23B SAM site and several groups of anti-aircraft guns had been positioned (*US DoD*)

Khark oil installations are shown in greater detail in this aerial photograph taken by the Americans. During the Iraqi offensives in 1984-85, the IrAF frequently targeted the two tanker jetties visible at the top of the shot, as well as their associated pipelines. The 61st TFW at Bushehr did its best to defend Khark, but the Iraqis not only had plans of the Iranian early warning radar net, but were also receiving increasing support from US and Saudi assets operating in the area (*US DoD*)

From the spring of 1984 Iraqi anti-shipping operations in the Khark area increased in ferocity, and the IRIAF was forced to step up combat air patrols over the Gulf. From May, F-4s also began attacking ships bound for Kuwait and Saudi Arabia, as both nations were actively supporting Iraq. This led to a series of clashes between Iranian and Saudi fighters, climaxing in the shooting down of a 61st TFW F-4E (flown by 1Lts Homayoun Hekmati and Cyrus Karimi) by RSAF F-15 Eagles on 5 June 1984. Both crewmen were killed. F-4E 3-6619 also belonged to the 61st TFW, and it is seen here passing low over a fully laden tanker heading south from Khark (*authors' collection*)

For it own anti-shipping strikes, the IRIAF experimentally equipped Phantom IIs with different weapons. These were mainly AGM-65A Mavericks and GP bombs, although Sidewinders were sometimes used. In late 1984 two F-4Es were also equipped to carry RIM-66A Standard SAMs in a makeshift anti-surface role. The results were disappointing, however, and the carriage of Standards was discontinued in early 1985 after only two or three ships had been attacked with them.

In March 1985 the Iranians struck the Iraqi defences at Basrah in an offensive known as *Badr*. The IrAF responded with fierce counterattacks, bombing numerous Iranian cities to begin what became known as the second round of the 'war of the cities' which had started a year earlier. The IrAF subsequently exploited the IRIAF's failure to field more than 50 fully operational F-4 Phantom IIs, along with a similar number of F-14s and F-5s, by hitting targets at will.

During the summer the Iraqis flew a series of heavy strikes against oil installations and tankers on Khark Island, but these raids were flown

By early 1986 heavy attrition had decreased the IRIAF's operational RF-4E force to just three jets. Due to their paucity in number, they were used only when intelligence was badly needed, as when Iran was preparing *Valfajr-8* – its most successful offensive into Iraq. In January 1986 two highly experienced IRIAF crews flew successful reconnaissance sorties along the southern part of the front, bringing back much vital information. This RF-4E is flying at extremely low level – note the hill-tops in the background rising above the Phantom II (*authors' collection*)

sporadically and lacked precision, resulting in no decisive damage being inflicted on Iran's crucial oil exports.

The IRIAF's Phantom II force began to experience better times in late 1985, when the Israelis made more covert deliveries of spare parts and weapons. These shipments were larger than ever before, and they enabled the Iranians to restore an increasing number of F-4Ds, F-4Es and RF-4Es to operability once again. Nevertheless, when the next major – and so far most successful – Iranian offensive into Iraq (Operation *Valfajr-8*) was initiated in February 1986, the IRIAF was largely held in reserve. Its air defence units were not, however, and during the offensive's opening days, the weather was so bad that SAM units – which had been completely reorganised in late 1985 – were mainly responsible for defending the ground forces against Iraqi air attack.

On 16 February, successful strikes were flown against three Iraqi air bases, and a number of helicopters and fighters were destroyed on the ground – two Phantom IIs were in turn badly damaged. F-4s from TFBs 3 and 4 subsequently flew numerous strikes against counter-attacking Iraqi ground units, using BL755s to inflict extensive losses.

In the air, Iranian fighters scrambled time and again to intercept a growing number of Iraqi strikes which were now supported by Egyptian Mirage 5SDEs equipped with Selenia ALQ-234 ECM pods. Numerous air combats developed, but the results were inconclusive due to heavy radar jamming employed by both sides. Even so, TFB 6 Phantom IIs claimed at least one Mirage 5SDE shot down by Sidewinders during an engagement in March for the loss of one or two F-4s to Iraqi air-to-air missiles over the western sector.

The IRIAF was initially held back during the early stages of Operation *Valfajr-8*, but once the IrAF started to launch counterattacks, the Iranians unleashed a series of strikes against Iraqi airfields near the front, claiming several fighters destroyed on the ground. This 71st TFW F-4D (3-6697) participated in these missions (*authors' collection*)

Legendary Iranian Phantom II pilot Maj Hossein Khalatbari poses with his F-4D. IRIAF Phantom IIs encountered Iraqi MiG-25s on several occasions, and during one engagement in February 1983, a single F-4E from TFB 3 surprised a MiG-25P escorting a MiG-25RB. A solitary AIM-7 was fired, but this went ballistic when the Phantom II had to break radar lock in order to avoid an R-40R missile fired at it by the MiG-25P. On 21 March 1986 Khalatbari was killed when his F-4D was shot down by Iraqi MiG-25Ps while on a mission over the frontline (*authors' collection*)

Over 95 per cent of Iranian losses came during operational missions, although the IrAF also kept the IRIAF constantly under pressure by attacking its bases. Marauding fighter-bombers sometimes managed to catch Iranian fighters exposed on the ground, including this F-4D which was destroyed by an Iraqi strike on Nojeh (TFB 3) in 1985 (*authors' collection*)

One of the aircraft lost was the F-4D flown by distinguished pilot, Maj Hossein Khalatbari. He was a respected commander and patriotic IRIAF Phantom II pilot who had flown both D- and E-models. He was also one of the top scorers with the Maverick missile, and together with Lt Col Dowran, Col Yassini and Capt Kian Sajedi, had played a key role in Operation *Morvarid*. Khalatbari was reportedly shot down by a long-range missile – probably an R-40 – fired by an Iraqi MiG-25PD during an engagement which also cost the Iraqis one aircraft.

THE BEGINNING OF THE END

In May 1986 Iranian Phantom IIs again raided IrAF bases along the central sector of the front in an attempt to hamper local counter-offensives. Meanwhile, as the IrAF was compelled to stop flying deep strikes into Iran and mount defensive CAPs instead, oil installations around Kirkuk were extensively bombed. For the rest of the year both sides concentrated on Iraqi anti-shipping operations in the Persian Gulf. On 12 July a single F-4E from Bushehr destroyed an Iraqi Super Frelon with an AGM-65A whilst the helicopter was parked on the al-Omayeh oil platform. When IrAF MiG-23s tried to intercept the Phantom II following this attack, one was shot down by a covering F-14. Then, on 11 August, four F-4Es from Nojeh bombed the ad-Dowrah oil refinery in southern Baghdad.

The Iraqis often attacked Iranian oil rigs in the Persian Gulf using Exocet missiles, this platform being hit in 1985. Although ignored in contemporary reports, the effectiveness of Iranian air defences increased from late 1985, and by the end of the war Phantom II crews had claimed a number of Iraqi fighters shot down over the Gulf (*authors' collection*)

The following month the IRIAF was largely grounded following a series of defections which were blamed on foreign intelligence

services. The pilots of two F-4s and one F-14A flew to Iraq, and these aircraft were destroyed following a detailed inspection by the Americans. Crewmembers who refused to be taken to the US for interrogation were handed over to the Iraqis, and they in turn treated them as prisoners of war. Worse was to come on 6 October when Capt Reza Mohamad, the highly respected CO of the 306th TFS (the F-4D detachment at Vahdati), was killed when his Phantom II was shot down in error by Iranian army air defences as he was landing at TFB 4.

By the autumn of 1986 the IrAF was using more modern Soviet-supplied equipment. This, combined with targeting intelligence sourced directly from the CIA, as well as the US Navy and Air Force, enabled Iraq to begin increasingly effective strikes against Iranian industrial infrastructure and oil installations in the Gulf. The IRIAF was relatively slow to react, and before long the IrAF was able to conduct several heavy bombing raids which almost halted Iranian oil exports.

In March 1985 the IrAF started operating Agave radar-equipped Mirage F 1EQ-5-200s which were capable of carrying Exocet missiles. Small numbers were used by the 91st Sqn at Kut al-Hayy, the 102nd Sqn at Qayyarah West and the 111th and 112th Sqns at Qayyarah South. The F 1s were used extensively during the war, although more than half those delivered were shot down by Iranian interceptors and air defences. Indeed, it is estimated that only six of the 20 F 1EQ-5s supplied to the IrAF survived the war (*Dassault Aviation via the authors*)

On 15 February 1986, two F-4Es that had been forward-deployed to TFB 4 flew a highly successful strike against the H-2 oil pumping station nearly 390 miles inside Iraq. However, after hitting their target the F-4s were intercepted by two Mirage F 1s and one of the Phantom IIs was shot down while still some 300 miles short of the Iranian border A daring rescue mission was successfully undertaken the very next morning, the crew being recovered by an IRIAF Pilatus PC-6B Turbo Porter, supported by diversionary attacks from several other Phantom IIs. The austere PC-6B proved indispensable during the war, frequently operating behind Iraqi lines recovering downed Iranian fliers (*authors' collection*)

By the late summer of 1987, IRIAF F-4Es were increasingly confronting US Navy fighters and surface ships in the Persian Gulf. On 8 August, two F-14As from VF-21 'Freelancers', embarked on the USS *Constellation* (CV 64), intercepted a 91st TFW F-4E, firing two Sparrows at it. The highly-experienced Phantom II crew evaded both missiles and avoided an engagement that they could hardly win, whilst the crew from one of the VF-21 jets came in for severe official criticism. These two 'Freelancers' F-14As were photographed at around the time the encounter took place (*via authors*)

In preparation for Operation *Karbala-8* – the 'final' Iranian offensive against Iraq – the IRIAF's trio of surviving RF-4Es were called on to supply vital photographic intelligence of Iraqi frontline positions. This photograph shows the Shatt al-Arab waterway, with the arrows pointing to the Um ol-Rassas Islet, which was subsequently used as a bridgehead by the IRGC (*authors' collection*)

From early 1987 the US Navy had also became more active in the Gulf, and its surveillance information helped the Iraqis to frustrate Operation *Karbala-5*, the next major Iranian offensive towards Basrah, which was initiated on 8 January.

Iranian Phantom IIs flew intensive missions in support of the new campaign, although improved Iraqi air defences limited them to hit-and-run close air support attacks directly along the frontline. But in co-operation with ground-based air defence units and F-14s, the Phantom II crews scored numerous air-to-air kills.

On 16 February two F-4Es from TFB 4 penetrated 400 miles into Iraq to hit the H-2 oil pumping station in the west of the country. As had happened many times before,

On 12 April 1988, two Phantom IIs from the 91st TFS attacked the United Arab Emirates' Mubarak oil rig in the lower Persian Gulf in revenge for a series of Iraqi air strikes against Iranian oil installations. The platform was badly damaged by several AGM-65As, and the Iranian government later apologised for this attack. The damage had been done, however, and Iran became increasingly isolated from the international community (*authors' collection*)

the IrAF was taken completely by surprise, although two Mirages managed to intercept the Phantom IIs as they headed back towards Iran, shooting one down some 312 miles inside Iraq. In a skilfully-organised combat search-and-rescue operation, the crew of the downed F-4E was recovered by an IRIAF Pilatus PC-6B the next day.

During the rest of 1987, the Phantom IIs flew mainly air defence sorties, frequently clashing with Iraqi strike formations which were increasing in size and intensity. They were also having to confront an increased US Navy presence in the Gulf. On 8 August, for example, an F-4E from Bushehr encountered two F-14As from VF-21, embarked on the USS *Constellation* (CV 64), which fired two Sparrows in response. One missile malfunctioned while the other was evaded by the battle-hardened Iranian crew.

By the autumn of 1987, Phantom IIs from Vahdati had been forced to defend their base, and surrounding guards and army ammunition depots, from fierce Iraqi air attacks. These strikes were led by Su-22s equipped with SPS-141 ECM pods and Kh-28M (AS-9) anti-radar missiles. The IRIAF pilots were swift to score, downing a MiG-23BN on 3 November, a MiG-21 the next day and a Mirage F 1EQ on 15 November. The new Sukhois proved exceptionally difficult to catch, however, although one was shot down by Phantom IIs on 17 November. Hawk SAM batteries claimed a MiG-23BN on 22 November, with a second jet being shot down by a Phantom II after a pursuit of almost 50 miles. A further two MiGs were also destroyed before the IrAF had to give up the chase. Despite the Iraqis achieving some successes during these strikes, the loss of one fighter and its pilot per sortie flown was too much for any air force to endure.

It was, however, clear by the spring of 1988 that Iran was barely capable of continuing the war. All of its 'decisive offensives' had so far failed, and efforts to mobilise a large new IRGC army to strike into Iraq had come to nothing.

Iranian C-130E/H Hercules aircraft like this one saw extensive service during the war. They directly supported F-4-equipped units by helping them move equipment, weapons and spare parts from one base to another. Such flights could be hazardous, as the serviceability of the Hercules fleet drastically decreased as the conflict ground on. In April 1988 a C-130 crashed near Bandar Abbas due to mechanical failure. All those aboard the transport were killed, most of the passengers being 91st TFW pilots transferring to the southern base from the north. The unit was effectively decimated just days prior to the IRIAF having to confront the US Navy during Operation *Praying Mantis* (authors' collection)

The Iranian Navy was badly mauled on 18 April 1988 during Operation *Praying Mantis*, which saw a series of strikes by US naval aircraft, launched from the USS *Enterprise* (CVN 65), sink two Iranian warships and damage another. In the air, Bandar Abbas-based P-3Fs and F-4Es that were sent to patrol the Strait of Hormuz were engaged by the US Navy, with an F-4E being damaged by two SM-2ER Standard missiles fired from the guided missile cruiser USS *Wainwright* (CG 28). The vessel's crew claimed the F-4 as shot down, although as this photos shows, the aircraft had only been damaged by the two SM-2ER SAMs. Later that day several Phantom IIs attempted to intercept an E-2C Hawkeye AEW aircraft, but they were frustrated in their efforts by the appearance of two F-14As from VF-213. The Iranian pilots had great respect for the Tomcat's long range firepower, and they did not risk engaging them (*US DoD*)

In May-June 1988, F-4Ds of the 71st TFW, deployed at four different bases in western Iran, participated in a series of fierce strikes against Iraqi air defences, forward airfields and artillery positions. For the Iranian F-4 Phantom II community, the war with Iraq ended almost as it had started – with a shock. This was due to two combat losses that resulted in the deaths of four crewmen. The first of these occurred on 14 June 1988, when Capt Salarie and his WSO from TFB 3 were killed during an aerial engagement with more than 50 Iraqi MiG-23s and Su-22s. The IrAF aircraft were responding to an IRIAF attack on Iraqi ground units in the Shalamcheh area. Further losses were suffered on 19 July, when an F-4E from TFB 6 was shot down by Iraqi Mirage F 1EQ-6s while searching for the crews of two F-14As which had reportedly been destroyed during a dogfight earlier in the day. This particular F-4D (3-6711) survived extensive damage to its undercarriage in October 1980, as well as further Iraqi AAA hits in 1981-82. The jet remains in service to this day (*authors' collection*)

After years of waiting for Iranian offensives, and making extensive preparations which completely changed their forces in 1986 and 1987, the Iraqis altered their stance. Encouraged by US intelligence assessments, they prepared a series of offensives which were intended not only to liberate territory held by Iran, but also to destroy the main Iranian army and IRGC units. The chief Iraqi objective was to throw the Iranians out of the Faw Peninsula, and a major operation, codenamed *Ramadhan al-Mubarak*, closely supported by the IrAF, was initiated at daybreak on 17 April 1988.

The Iraqis advanced swiftly, and the weak Iranian garrison retreated after being partially overrun. Many men had to swim across the Shatt al-Arab waterway to escape, and once again the IRGC commanders started calling on the 'useless' IRIAF for help. By noon, the first Iranian jets appeared over Faw, forcing several Iraqi formations to turn away without attacking Iranian positions. The CO of TFB 6, Col Alireza Yassini, then started sending one formation after another to bomb advancing Iraqi forces, and to intercept raiding aircraft. The Phantom II units at Bushehr sortied aircraft every ten minutes until sunset on the 17th, Yassini himself flying two combat missions that day.

He later recalled that on one sortie he had tried to fly towards the rear of an Iraqi troop column in order to bomb it, but that to his consternation

he could not find the end of it! Yassini finally released his bombs, but with very little obvious effect.

The opening day of this new offensive signalled the beginning of the end of the long and bloody Iran-Iraq War. However, neither side was ready to stop fighting just yet. The Iranians attempted to halt the invasion by launching a series of local counter-offensives.

IRIAF Phantom IIs were sent aloft on an increasing number of strikes deep into Iraq, hitting oil installations, and engaging in air-to-air combats in April and May 1988. Several Mirage F 1EQs, MiG-23BNs and Su-22s were shot down. Su-25s were also encountered, albeit inconclusively. A few painful losses were suffered by the Iranians as well, and on 14 June Capt Salarie was shot down and killed when eight Iranian fighters encountered over 50 Iraqi aircraft in the Shalamcheh area. Fighting for his life, Salarie destroyed a MiG-23 just prior to his demise.

On 19 July – the very day the Iranian government accepted United Nations Resolution 598, calling for a ceasefire – an F-4E from Bushehr was shot down by an Iraqi Mirage F 1EQ using newly-delivered Super 530D air-to-air missiles. The aircraft was apparently one of a number of IRIAF jets searching for the crews of two F-14As reported as having been shot down by Mirages earlier in the day.

That same afternoon F-4s flew some of the last combat sorties of the war when they attacked targets deep in Iraq. These strikes on heavily-defended targets in Baghdad and Kirkuk proved that the Phantom II force was still capable of penetrating enemy airspace and hitting targets of its choice, despite Iraq's deployment of what was considered to be one of the world's best air-defence systems, to say nothing of advanced fighters like the MiG-29.

EPILOGUE

The three versions of the Phantom II used by the IRIAF saw extensive service during the war with Iraq. In fact, F-4-equipped units flew as many sorties during the first two years of the conflict as they did in the remaining six. The reason for this is simple – the IRIAF fought fiercely to halt the Iraqis and expel the invaders from Iran. Once this was accomplished, the air force was conserved as a 'force in being'. For the rest of the war, the IRIAF continued to fight, and indeed did so intensively, but the preservation of its remaining assets was the overriding priority. And this policy paid off, for the Phantom II still forms the backbone of the IRIAF today.

All three versions of the F-4 Phantom II delivered to Iran remain in service and form the backbone of Iranian airpower as this volume goes to press. This four-ship formation was photographed during a fly-past conducted shortly after the end of the war with Iraq (*authors' collection*)

APPENDICES

KNOWN AERIAL VICTORIES SCORED BY PHANTOM II CREWS DURING THE IRAN-IRAQ WAR

date	location	version	pilot	WSO	unit	weapon	opponent	aircrew
9 Sep 80	-	F-4E	-	-	TFB 3	-	MiG-21R	-
14 Sep 80	S Pol-e Zahab	F-4E	-	-	TFB 3	AIM-9P-1	MiG-21R	-
14 Sep 80	S Pol-e Zahab	F-4E	-	-	TFB 3	AIM-9P-1	MiG-21MF	-
22 Sep 80	Tehran	F-4E	-	-	TFB 1	-	MiG-23BN	Egyptian
22 Sep 80	Tehran	F-4E	-	-	TFB 1	-	MiG-23BN	-
22 Sep 80	B Mosharaf	F-4E	-	-	TFB 6	AIM-9P-1	Su-22	-
22 Sep 80	B Mosharaf	F-4E	-	-	TFB 6	AIM-9P-1	Su-22	-
22 Sep 80	B Mosharaf	F-4E	-	-	TFB 6	AIM-9P-1	Su-22	-
23 Sep 80	Gayyarah air base	F-4E	-	-	TFB 3	20 mm	MiG-21MF	-
23 Sep 80	Sanandaj	F-4E	-	-	TFB 3	-	Su-22	-
23 Sep 80	Khabodar-Ahang	F-4E	-	-	TFB 3	-	MiG-21MF	-
24 Sep 80	Islam Abad West	F-4E	-	-	-	-	MiG-21MF	-
24 Sep 80	Islam Abad West	F-4E	-	-	-	-	MiG-21MF	-
24 Sep 80	Islam Abad West	F-4E	-	-	-	-	Su-20	-
24 Sep 80	Islam Abad West	F-4E	-	-	-	-	MiG-21MF	-
24 Sep 80	Islam Abad West	F-4E	-	-	-	-	MiG-21MF	-
24 Sep 80	Khark	F-4E	-	-	TFB 6	-	MiG-23BN	-
24 Sep 80	Khark	F-4E	-	-	TFB 6	-	MiG-23BN	-
24 Sep 80	Khark	I-4E	-	-	TFB 6	-	MiG-23BN	-
25 Sep 80	Al-Hurriya air base	F-4E	-	-	TFB 3	20 mm	Hunter F 59	-
25 Sep 80	Baghdad	F-4E	-	-	TFB 1	AIM-9P-1	MiG-21MF	-
25 Sep 80	Baghdad	F-4E	-	-	TFB 1	AIM-9P-1	MiG-21MF	-
25 Sep 80	Baghdad	F-4E	-	-	TFB 1	AIM-9P-1	MiG-21MF	-
28 Sep 80	-	F-4E	-	-	TFB 6	AIM-7E-2	MiG-23BN	-
29 Sep 80	Masjed Soleiman	F-4E	-	-	TFB 6	AIM-9P-1	MiG-21MF	-
29 Sep 80	Abadan	F-4E	-	-	TFB 6	AIM-9P-1	Su-22	-
29 Sep 80	Abadan	F-4E	-	-	TFB 6	AIM-9P-1	Su-22	-
29 Sep 80	Abadan	F-4E	-	-	TFB 6	AIM-9P-1	Su-22	-
2 Oct 80	-	F-4E	-	-	TFB 6	AIM-9P-1	MiG-23MS	-
10 Oct 80	Baghdad	F-4E	-	-	TFB 3	AIM-9P-1	MiG-21MF	-
14 Oct 80	-	F-4E	-	-	TFB 3	-	MiG	-
17 Oct 80	Baghdad	F-4E	-	-	TFB 3	20 mm	MiG-21MF	-
17 Oct 80	Baghdad	F-4E	-	-	TFB 3	20 mm	MiG-21MF	-
23 Oct 80	Abadan	F-4E	-	-	TFB 3	-	MiG-21MF	-
6 Nov 80	Tabriz	F-4E	-	-	TFB 3	AIM-9P-1	MiG-21MF	-
Nov 80	-	F-4E	Siavash Bayani	-	TFB 1	AIM-9P-1	Mi-25	-
29 Nov 80	Al-Omayeh	F-4E	-	-	TFB 6	AIM-9P-1	MiG-23	-
19 Dec 80	-	F-4E	-	-	TFB 6	-	Su-20	-
19 Dec 80	-	F-4E	-	-	TFB 6	-	Su-20	-
?? Dec 80	-	F-4E	Afkhami	-	TFB 1	-	MiG-21MF	-
21 Jan 81	-	F-4E	A Hoda	-	TFB 3	AIM-9P-1	MiG-23	-
24 Jan 81	-	F-4E	A Hoda	-	TFB 3	20 mm	MiG-23	-
25 Apr 81	S Pol-e Zahab	F-4E	Sarlack	-	TFB 3	20 mm	MiG-21MF	Dinmaruf
26 Apr 81	U'Ibn-Jarrah	F-4E	Mahloudji	Goudarz	TFB 3	AIM-9P-1	MiG-21MF	-
26 Apr 81	U Ibn-Jarrah	F-4E	Abbasi	Kutchmeshghi	TFB 3	AIM-9P-1	MiG-23MS	-
15 May 81	Vahdati	F-4E	-	-	TFB 3	AIM-9P-1	MiG-21MF	-
1 Sep 81	Shalamcheh	F-4D	-	-	TFB 7	AIM-7E-2	MiG-23MS	-
22 Sep 81	-	F-4E	Mofidi	-	TFB 3	AIM-9P-1	MiG-21MF	-
19 Mar 82	Dezful	F-4E	-	-	TFB 3	AIM-9P-1	MiG-21MF	-
4 Apr 82	Baghdad	F-4E	-	-	TFB 3	AIM-9P-1	MiG-21MF	-
22 Apr 82	Baghdad	F-4E	-	-	TFB 1	AIM-9P-1	An-24TV	-
28 Aug 82	Nasseriyah	F-4E	-	-	TFB 3	AIM-9P-1	An-24TV	-
15 Jul 82	Shalamcheh	F-4E	-	-	TFB 3	AIM-9P-1	MiG-21MF	-
15 Sep 82	Vahdati	F-4E	-	-	TFB 3	AIM-9P-1	MiG-21MF	-

date	location	version	pilot	WSO	unit	weapon	opponent	aircrew
Oct 82	M Ibn-Aqil TO	F-4E	-	-	TFB 3	AIM-9P-1	Su-20	-
Oct 82	M Ibn-Aqil TO	F-4E	-	-	TFB 3	AIM-9P-1	MiG-23MS	-
16 Nov 82	Moharram TO	F-4E	-	-	TFB 3	AIM-9P-1	MiG-21MF	-
20 Nov 82	Moharram TO	F-4E	-	-	TFB 3	AIM-9P-1	MiG-23	-
21 Nov 82	Moharram TO	F-4E	-	-	TFB 3	AIM-9P-1	Su-20 or Su-22	-
13 Mar 83	-	F-4E	-	-	TFB 3	AIM-7E-2	Su-22M-3K	-
4 May 83	-	F-4E	A Hoda	-	TFB 3	AIM-9P-1	Su-22	-
16 Jun 83	-	F-4E	Siavash Bayani	-	TFB 1	AIM-9P-1	Mi-25	R Geschke
2 Apr 84	Khark	F-4E	Adibi	-	TFB 6	AIM-7E-2	Super Etendard	-
29 Apr 84	Khark	F-4E	-	-	TFB 6	AIM-9P-1	MiG-23	-
14 Jan 85	Khark	F-4E	-	-	TFB 6	-	-	-
9 Mar 85	Baghdad	F-4E	-	-	TFB 3	-	-	-
11 Mar 85	Baladruz	F-4E	-	-	TFB 3	AIM-9P-1	MiG-23MS	-
15 Mar 85	Tigris	F-4E	-	-	TFB 4	AIM-9P-1	MiG-23BK	-
19 Apr 85	Howeizeh	F-4E	A Hoda	-	TFB 3	-	MiG-21bis	-
??/??/85	-	F-4E	-	-	TFB 1	manœuvre	MiG-23MF	-
10 Feb 86	Faw	F-4E	-	-	TFB 6	AAM	Mirage F 1EQ	-
14 Feb 86	al-Omayeh	F-4E	-	-	TFB 6	AIM-7?	SA 321GV	-
?? Mar 85	Faw	F-4E	-	-	TFB 6	AIM-9P-1	Mirage 5SDE	-
15 Aug 86	Khark	F-4E	-	-	TFB 6	AIM-9P-1	Su-22	-
15 Aug 86	Khark	F-4E	-	-	TFB 6	20 mm	Su-22	-
15 Nov 86	-	F-4E	A Hoda	-	TFB 3	AIM-9P-1	MiG-23	-
17 Nov 87	Dezful	F-4E	-	-	TFB 3	AIM-9P-1	Su-22M-3K	-
22 Nov 87	Dezful	F-4E	-	-	TFB 3	AIM-9P-1	MiG-23BN	-
25 Nov 87	Dezful	F-4E	-	-	TFB 3	AIM-9P-1	Su-22M-3K	-
6 Mar 88	-	F-4E	A Hoda	-	TFB 3	AIM-9P-1	Mirage F 1EQ	-
19 Mar 88	-	F-4E	-	-	TFB 6	AIM-7E-2	Tu-22B	-
8 May 88	-	F-4E	-	-	TFB 3	20 mm	Su-22M-4K	-
14 Jun 88	Shalamcheh	F-4E	Salarie	-	TFB 3	AIM-9P-1	MiG-23MS	-
25 Jul 88	-	F-4E	-	-	TFB ?	20 mm	Bell 412ST	-

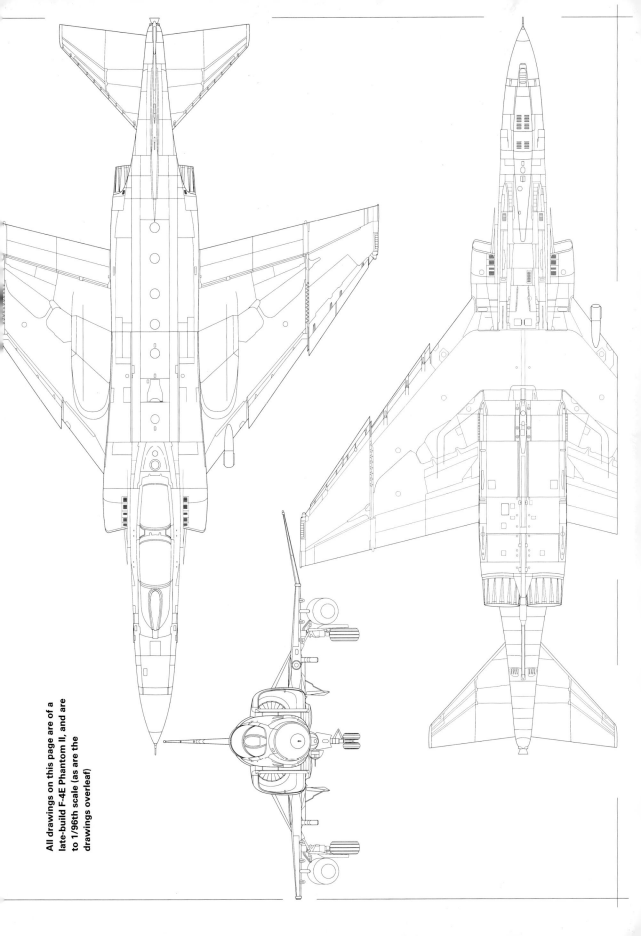

All drawings on this page are of a late-build F-4E Phantom II, and are to 1/96th scale (as are the drawings overleaf)

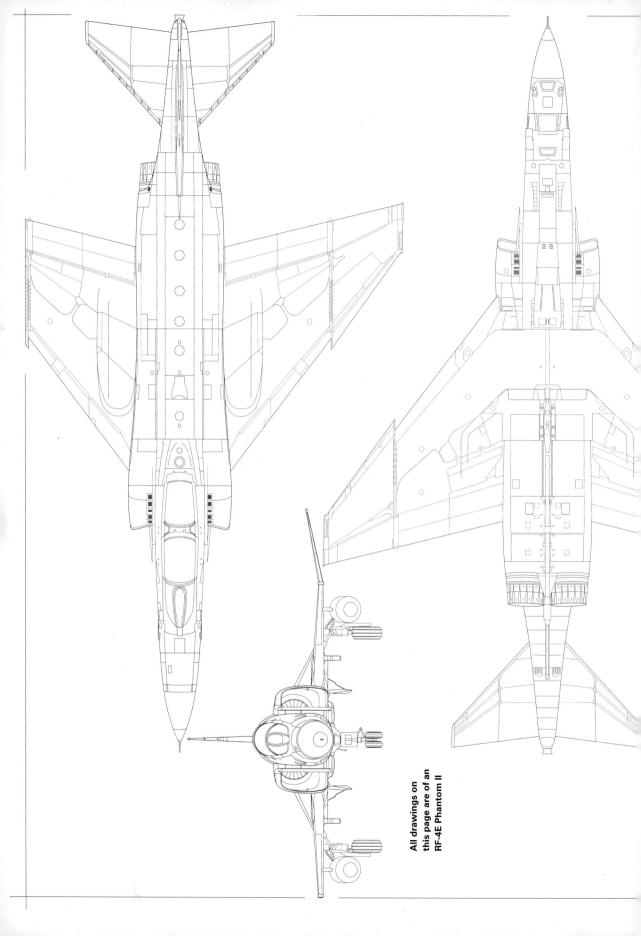

All drawings on
this page are of an
RF-4E Phantom II

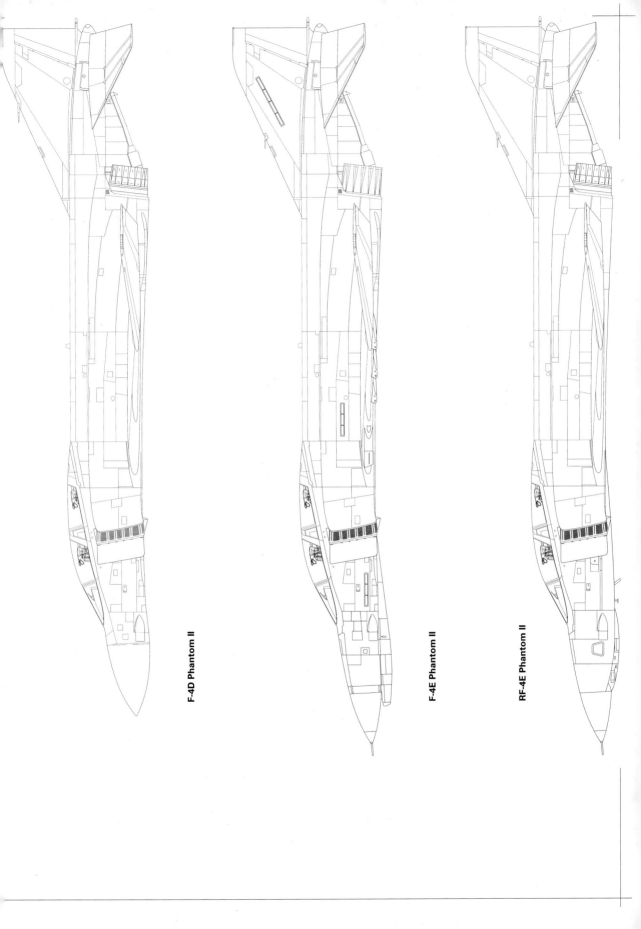

F-4D Phantom II

F-4E Phantom II

RF-4E Phantom II

1
F-4D 67-14879 (formerly 3-601 and 3-663) 3-6697 of the 71st TFW, 29 September 1980

In October 1980 this particular F-4D joined two other Phantom IIs from the 71st TFW in a bridge-busting mission south-west of Basrah. It was one of two F-4 'target-busters', which relied on a third, higher-flying Phantom II to designate the bridge with its AN/AVQ-9 'Zot Box' (note the 'black box' in the aircraft's rear cockpit). The operation went smoothly and the target was destroyed, although the designator aircraft was downed by an SA-6 SAM – the crew ejected safely. 67-14879 also served with the 32nd and 61st TFWs during the war, and is still in IRIAF service today.

2
F-4D 67-14881 3-6699 of the 71st TFW, October 1980

Due to the fact that Iranian F-4Ds received new serials at least twice, the original Fiscal Year number for this particular Phantom II remains unknown. The jet saw extensive service during the war, despite being badly damaged during an attack with GP bombs on Iraqi troops in southern Khuzestan in October 1980. Damaged again in combat three years later, 3-6711 was repaired once more and returned to full operational status in 1984. The veteran fighter-bomber also served with the 32nd, 61st and 91st TFWs, and ultimately survived the war.

3
F-4D 67-14800 3-6713 of the 71st TFW, October 1980

Although only 15 of the 30 IRIAF F-4Ds in service in September 1980 eventually survived the war, contrary to many reports in the western press, they were never used as spares sources to keep F-4Es flying. The F-4Ds remained the fastest Phantom IIs in Iranian service, thanks to their highly experienced ground-support personnel. Note that this jet is fitted with an ALQ-87(V)-4 ECM pod in the forward left Sparrow missile trough. This bolt-on system was employed with considerable success right up until the end of the war. 3-6713 was one of the 15 F-4Ds to survive the conflict.

4
F-4D 68-????? 3-6716 of the 32nd TFW, April 1981

In early 1979 (just prior to the revolution) the IIAF purchased four RHAWS upgrading kits for its F-4Ds, and 3-6716 was one of the quartet of Phantom II to be modified. Following the upgrade, the aircraft was used extensively as a deep strike leader, as on 4 April 1981 when nine F-4s bombed H-3 air base in western Iraq, destroying numerous fighters and bombers on the ground. 3-6716 was also equipped with an ALQ-101 ECM pod and BL 755 CBUs for this mission. Delivered in 1970, the aircraft also served with the 71st TFW. Its final fate remains unknown

5
F-4E 69-077?? 3-6570 of the 31st TFW, 21 July 1982

Delivered in 1972, this Phantom II was flown on its final mission, on 21 July 1982, by Lt Col Abbas Dowran and Capt Mansour Kazemiyan. Sent to attack the National Conference Centre in Baghdad, the aircraft was armed with two heavy Mk 84 GP bombs and an ALQ-87 ECM pod. Theoretically, the IRIAF could have used GBU-10-armed F-4Ds, but such an attack would have required one of the Phantom IIs to fly high and steady, guiding the LGBs to the target, and thus exposing it to AAA and SAMs. Dowran, therefore, decided to perform a fast, low-level attack in which the Mk 84s – the only bombs heavy enough to damage the large complex – would be dropped during a high-speed pass, as he saw no other way of surviving the mission. The plan was frustrated by low-altitude Roland SAMs, which shot 3-6570 down short of its intended target. This aircraft had also saw service with the 32nd TFW prior to flying with the 31st TFW.

6
F-4E 71-01??? 3-6591 of the 11th TFW, September 1980

During the war with Iraq, Iranian F-4Es added at least 90 (and probably as many as 120) aerial kills to the already impressive records achieved by US and Israeli Phantom IIs. In the autumn of 1980, 11th TFW F-4Es saw extensive air combat, both during raids into Iraq and in the defence of Iran. This particular Phantom II flew 40+ sorties deep into Iraq, and scored at least three aerial kills Its final fate is unknown.

7
F-4E 71-01??? 3-6605 of the 61st TFW, 22 September 1980

3-6605 and three other F-4Es from TFB 6 flew the IRIAF's first combat sorties of the war when they carried out a successful surprise attack on Iraq's Shoaibah air base, near Basrah, on the afternoon of 22 September 1980. This aircraft was one of the first F-4Es delivered to Iran, and it was later modified with leading-edge slats during the mid-1970s. The aircraft's final fate is unknown.

8
F-4E 71-01??? 3-6611 of the 31st TFW, January 1981

While supporting a naval raid against Iraqi oil rigs in the northern Persian Gulf on 29 November 1980, Maverick-armed IRIAF F-4Es wrought havoc on the Iraqi Navy, destroying almost all of its Osa-I and Osa-II missile boats, as well other vessels participating in the raid, using AGM-65A Mavericks. TISEO-equipped 3-6611 was one of the F-4Es involved in this operation, the jet serving with both the 31st and 61st TFWs. Its final fate is unknown.

9
F-4E 71-01??? 3-6612 of the 61st TFW, October 1980
On 17 October 1980, this jet, and a second
F-4E, participated in a raid against an Iraqi
motorised unit staging area near Khoramshahr.
During the course of the attack, it was hit in
the tail section by a SAM, causing the WSO
to inadvertently eject and be killed. The pilot
managed to make a safe emergency landing back
at Bushehr, however. 3-6612 was subsequently
repaired, although it is not known if it survived
the war.

10
F-4E 73-0154? 3-6616 of the 61st TFW, October 1980
3-6616 participated in an early-war strike on the
Iraqi Umm Qassr naval base, during which
numerous ships were sunk. The Phantom II was
badly damaged by an SA-6, although the pilot
managed to fly the jet safely back to base. The
aircraft is shown here carrying M-117 GP bombs
on triple-ejector racks (TERs) attached to the inner
underwing pylons. The IRIAF made extensive use
of M-117s during the war, developing retarding
fins for them. 3-6616 survived the war.

11
F-4E 73-015?? 3-6629 of the 31st TFW, November 1980
On 19 November 1980, 3-6629 was one of four
Phantom IIs sent to attack the football stadium at
Badreh, which Iraq was using as a staging area for
army helicopters. One of the F-4Es was shot down
and its crew captured, but the other three returned
safely. 3-6629 served with the 31st and 32nd TFWs
at TFB 3, although its final fate is unknown

12
F-4E 73-01544 3-6642 of the 32nd TFW, October/November 1982
3-6642 was one of the most famous of all TFB 3
F-4Es, the jet flying 1000+ combat sorties between
1980 and 1988. It is also known to have downed at
least two MiGs. The aircraft is shown here carrying
a maximum bombload of six Mk 82s, fitted with
Mk 15 Snakeye retarding fins, on the multiple
ejector rack (MER) under the centreline, and three
more bombs on single TERs attached to each inner
underwing pylon. Together with two drop tanks
(deleted here in order to show bombload details),
and two Sparrows in the rear bays, this payload
was one of the heftiest carried by Iranian Phantom
IIs during the war. 3-6642 served with both the
31st and 32nd TFWs at TFB 3, and its final fate
is unknown.

13
F-4E 73-01545 3-6643 of the 32nd TFW, summer 1982
During the summer and autumn of 1982, the 31st
and 32nd TFWs, based at TFB 3, flew missions in
support of Iranian ground offensives along the
central sector of the front with Iraq. IRIAF Phantom
IIs destroyed more than 100 Iraqi tanks, using

mainly napalm fire bombs and unguided rockets,
during the course of these operations. 3-6643 is
known to have participated in these strikes, and
to have survived the war. It is shown here
carrying LAU-61 Folding-Fin Aircraft Rocket pods
(containing 19 70 mm calibre rockets per tube)
mounted in pairs on TERs affixed to the inboard
pylons.

14
F-4E 73-01547 3-6645 of the 61st TFW, summer 1982
TISEO-equipped 3-6645 was flown by Maj Yassini
during several of his highly successful missions
using Maverick missiles, including the sortie on
29 November 1980 when he sank several Iraqi Osa
missile boats. Two years later, the jet was used
mainly to support Iranian army units in their
offensives in south-western Iran. The IRIAF
made extensive use of napalm during this
campaign, and 3-6645 is shown here carrying
BLU-27 napalm-filled fire bombs (without tail fins).
The aircraft survived the war.

15
F-4E 73-01548 3-6646 of the 61st TFW, May 1984
Armed exclusively with air-to-air missiles, the 61st
TFW's Phantom IIs were tasked with defending
Iranian oil tankers and merchant shipping from
IrAF Exocet missile attacks, and between 1982 and
1988 they scored a number of kills against Iraqi
Super Etendards and Mirages over the Persian
Gulf. Note the strike camera (rectangular in shape)
mounted where the wings and the fuselage meet
on this jet. Almost all Iranian F-4s were equipped
with two such cameras, and these proved their
worth not only by recording the results of
bombing attacks on targets, but also by providing
up to the minute reconnaissance footage. This
aircraft survived the war.

16
F-4E 73-01552 3-6650 of the 11th TFW, February 1986
3-6650 participated in the successful Iranian
offensives of February 1986, which brought
the Iraqi army to the brink of collapse. It flew
numerous attacks on the IrAF's forward airfields,
during which a number of fighters and helicopters
were destroyed on the ground. 3-6650 survived
the war. Note that it boasts a rarely seen
underwing roundel.

17
F-4E 75-02453 3-6681 of the 11th TFW, May 1988
3-6681 was operated by the 91st TFW until it was
sent to Mehrabad (in 1982) and then to Bushehr,
where the Phantom II was used for testing several
different modifications, including the installation of
the Shahin rocket, seen in this illustration. The
Shahin was an unguided weapon of large calibre,
developed in Iran and introduced to service in
1982. This aircraft was used as a launch platform
for a Shahin rocket attack on the Kirkuk oil refinery

in 1982, the jet being flown by Lt Col Abbas Dowran, with 1Lt Turaj Dehghani as his WSO. This was one of the first missions on which the missile was employed, and diving at an angle of 35 degrees, Dowran fired two Shahins from 2000 ft. Both scored direct hits, creating huge fireballs. Leaving the target area, the Phantom II was intercepted by two MiGs and damaged by AAA, although Dowran managed to make it safely back to base. The Shahin was to see extensive service, especially in the spring of 1988. This F-4 served with both the 91st and 11th TFWs, and survived the war

18
F-4E 75-02??? 3-6684 of the 32nd TFW, 1986
TISEO-equipped 3-6684 was one of the F-4Es forward-deployed to TFB 4 by the 32nd TFW for much of the war. Known to be a reliable jet, it was a favourite with several pilots, and was used to shoot down at least one MiG-21. The aircraft is shown here carrying a load of Mk 82 GP bombs (equipped with Mk 15 Snakeye retarding fins) and Sidewinders attached to its inner underwing pylons, two Sparrows in the rear missile troughs and an ALQ-87 ECM pod in the forward right Sparrow trough. Such combinations were needed for missions flown into areas where heavier resistance from IrAF fighters had to be expected, this configuration usually being reserved for flight leaders only. 3-6684 served with the 91st and 32nd TFWs at TFB 9, and survived the war

19
F-4E 75-0250 3-6691 of the 91st TFW, March 1985
TISEO-equipped 3-6691 was one of two F-4Es from the 91st TFS (nicknamed 'The Sharks') which were modified to carry and fire RIM-66 Standard surface-to-air missiles, taken from Iranian Navy destroyers, in the air-launched anti-shipping role. On 27 February 1984, after three test launches from Phantom IIs, one was fired at the 255,557-ton Greek tanker *Captain John G P Livanos*, sailing some 170 nautical miles north-east of Dubai en route to Khark Island. The missile caused very little damage to its target, and the attack highlighted numerous problems associated with using the weapon in this way. Although the Standards were used on two subsequent anti-shipping strikes, the idea was eventually dropped. This aircraft served with both the 91st and 61st TFWs, and survived the war

20
RF-4E UKI 2-650 of the 61st TFW, February 1986
RF-4E 2-6504 was one of the jets labelled an Unknown Iranian, hence the UKI designation. It was delivered to Iran in the 1970s directly from the USAF for clandestine joint US-Iranian reconnaissance operations beyond the Soviet borders. It was also the only Iranian RF-4E known to have had its undersides painted black. The aircraft was last seen in February 1986 at Bushehr (TFB 6), where it was based whilst undertaking a

series of reconnaissance sorties in preparation for the Iranian offensive Operation *Valfajr-8*. It final fate remains unknown.

21
RF-4E 74-17?? 2-6510 of the 11th TFW, 1987
This aircraft is one of only nine Iranian RF-4Es known to have survived the conflict with Iraq – by war's end only three of these airframes were actually operational. Being extremely capable reconnaissance platforms, they were highly valued by the Iranians, and the jets supplied intelligence for most kinds of military operation. 2-6510 flew hundreds of extremely risky missions, and participated in the joint Iranian-Israeli operation which led to the successful strikes on Iraq's nuclear reactor in 1980-81. The first of these missions was flown by IRIAF F-4Es on 30 September 1980 and the second by Israeli air force jets on 6 June 1981. This aircraft served with both the 61st and 11th TFWs.

COLOUR SECTION

1
Between 1977 and late 1978, the IIAF received its final batches of F-4Es, totalling 36 aircraft in all. These Phantom IIs were some of the best-equipped F-4Es ever built for any air force. This pre-delivery photograph of 75-0250, taken in St Louis, shows that the aircraft was fitted with both a TISEO (target identification electro-optical) fairing near the left wing root and leading edge slats (LES) (*McDonnell Douglas/Boeing via authors*)

2
Pilots and officers of the 31st TFW pose with an F-4E at Shahrokhi (TFB 3) in 1977 (*authors' collection*)

3
During the course of October 1980, IRIAF's two F-4D squadrons lost no fewer than six aircraft in combat, and had three more badly damaged. Such was the price for flying laser-guided bombing missions which delivered heavy blows against the Iraqis, but which in turn exposed the Phantom IIs to enemy air defences. This example survived a major in flight fire caused by a series of AAA hits, the jet returning to Vahdati air base with much of its forward fuselage burnt out. Despite having been seriously damaged, the aircraft was duly repaired and returned to service (*authors' collection*)

4
F-4D 3-6713 is seen just seconds after taking off from Vahdati air base. The IRIAF applied fresh serials to all the Phantom IIs that it inherited from the IIAF at least twice between 1979 and 1981, so the exact construction number of this example –

which survived the war after flying hundreds of combat sorties – remains unknown (*authors' collection*)

5

An F-4E carrying six Mk 82s (equipped with Mk 15 Snakeye retarding fins) closes on the extended flying boom deployed from a Boeing 707-3J9C tanker. Aerial refuelling was commonplace for IRIAF fighter-bombers prior to them pressing on into Iraq. The use of Snakeyes enabled Iranian Phantom II crews to drop their weapons precisely from very low levels and at very high speeds (*authors' collection*)

6

Operation *Howeizeh*, launched by the Iranians on 5 January 1981, saw some of the fiercest armoured fighting of the war, and IRIAF F-4Es flew many strikes in support of ground forces, firing literally dozens of AGM-65As. The first Iranian offensive of the conflict, *Howeizeh* was marred by intelligence failures, resulting in it being ultimately less successful than it might otherwise have been (*authors' collection*)

7

Examples of the three main IRIAF fast jet aircraft types used during the Iran-Iraq War are seen in this flypast over Tehran's Azadi (Shahyad) Square. Formating behind the extended flying boom and wingtip drogues of a Boeing 707-3J9C tanker are an F-5E Tiger II, RF-4E Phantom II and an F-14A Tomcat (*authors' collection*)

8

For much of the Iran-Iraq War, the IRIAF lacked an effective anti-shipping missile. In an effort to solve this serious shortcoming, the 61st and 91st TFWs joined forces with the 'Self-Sufficiency Task Force (Jihad)', which was a team organised by IRIAF technicians and IACI engineers, and supported by various universities. Several possible solutions were experimented with, including the mounting of a RIM-66A Standard surface-to-air missile taken from the Navy's *Badr* class (formerly US *Gearing* class) destroyers on the outer wing pylons of two 61st TFW Phantom IIs, including 75-0250/3-6691. Trials with this 'new' weapon were undertaken in the autumn of 1984, and problems soon arose with the missile's guidance system, which was never properly interfaced with the aircraft's weapons guidance equipment. The experiment was subsequently cancelled, although an increased number of Iraqi Exocet missile attacks on tankers in the Persian Gulf eventually forced the IRIAF to use the Phantom II/Standard combination on at least three anti-shipping strikes in late 1985. Despite the technical problems, hits were still achieved with two of the weapons (*authors' collection*)

9

Although the number of serviceable F-4Es available for Persian Gulf patrols had steadily dwindled by 1986, the 61st TFW nevertheless continued to keep the Iranian tanker-shuttle between Khark and the lower Persian Gulf open. The wing also successfully defended an increasing number of ships transporting weapons to Iran from Israel. Between September 1980 and July 1988, less than two per cent of ships passing along the Iranian coast were hit by Iraqi air strikes. IRIAF Phantom IIs like F-4E 3-6643, seen here passing low over a super tanker, were largely responsible for protecting these vessels (*authors' collection*)

10

The subject of colour profile 1, F-4D 3-6697 is seen landing at Chabahar (TFB 10) in late 1980. Note the TFB 10 symbol on the tail, this airfield housing the maintenance and overhaul centre for all IRIAF Phantom IIs. This aircraft was fitted with an AN/AVQ-9 'Zot Box' in its rear cockpit, making it a key asset in the delivery of LGBs (*authors' collection*)

11 & 12

A TISEO- and LES-equipped F-4E from TFB 6 patrols the Persian Gulf in the mid 1980s, the aircraft being configured exclusively as an interceptor. It is carrying two AIM-7E-2 Sparrow missiles in the rear fuselage missile troughs and single AIM-9J/P-1 Sidewinders on the two inner wing pylons – a typical weapons fit for F-4Es involved in the tanker war. The Iranians purchased several hundred AIM-7E-2 rounds both before and during the war, and the IRIAF used them continuously with some success, despite the usual problems associated with the weapon's reliability (*both authors' collection*)

INDEX